The Thief
in the Classroom

The Thief
in the Classroom

How School Funding
Is Misdirected, Disconnected,
and Ideologically Aligned

Jeff Swensson, Lynn Lehman, and John Ellis

ROWMAN & LITTLEFIELD
Lanham • Boulder • New York • London

Published by Rowman & Littlefield
An imprint of The Rowman & Littlefield Publishing Group, Inc.
4501 Forbes Boulevard, Suite 200, Lanham, Maryland 20706
www.rowman.com

6 Tinworth Street, London SE11 5AL, United Kingdom

British Library Cataloguing in Publication Information Available

Library of Congress Cataloging-in-Publication Data

ISBN 978-1-4758-6027-6 (cloth: alk. paper)
ISBN 978-1-4758-6028-3 (pbk.: alk. paper)
ISBN 978-1-4758-6029-0 (electronic)

♾™ The paper used in this publication meets the minimum requirements of
American National Standard for Information Sciences—Permanence of Paper
for Printed Library Materials, ANSI/NISO Z39.48-1992.

Contents

Preface   vii

Introduction   1

1 Dollars and Sense: The Basics of Public School Funding for Educational Programs   3

2 Grab Bag Funding: Promises, Problems, and Prizes   15

3 A Case Study: Weeds in Indiana's School Funding Field   31

4 What Does School Funding Pay for?   45

5 Are We Really Paying for What We Get?   63

6 Public Education Is a Test   77

7 The Magic and the Consequences of School Funding   93

8 The Thief in the Classroom   109

9 Funding for Public Education: Is There a Bottom Line?   123

10 To Catch a Thief   139

References   155

Index   167

About the Authors   171

Preface

The authors of this book are veteran public school educators with experience in urban, suburban, and rural school districts throughout the Midwest. For us, regardless of the role we played in our school district, funding had a student-centric purpose: dynamic instruction. As is true for most public educators, it did not take us a long time to figure out two things about this purpose.

First, to the surprise of no one, dynamic instruction requires robust and adequate funding. To engage all students with professionally trained teachers throughout wide-ranging subject areas that offer challenging learning experiences including numerous lab courses is a worthwhile and revenue-intensive proposition.

Second, to our genuine surprise, there is a most unlikely thief lurking in classrooms in the United States: funding for public education. Inadequate funding for public education, it turns out, steals the promises of traditional public education.

Generated by often byzantine formulas concocted and implemented by state legislatures, revenue for public education shapes the future of millions of students in the United States. Theft in the classroom results when funding is inequitable and inadequate.

These revelations are important but largely ignored beyond the world of public education. This is because funding for public education is elaborate, complicated, and boring. It's a topic unlikely to command frequent public discussion. Funding for public education, nevertheless, holds the key to the future for US students and, thus, for the nation as a whole.

The purpose of this book is to put in focus the contemporary disparities and future possibilities of funding for US public education. Present-day, adult-centric funding is responsible for disparities that shortchange all US students. Student-centric funding represents the as-yet unrealized promises of traditional public education.

This book puts school funding and its everyday importance to teaching and learning into perspective. Educators, parents, caregivers, and policymakers can use this narrative to track down the thief in the classroom. By identifying what is stolen and by establishing the need to understand the damage done by contemporary school funding formulas, this discussion reveals why funding for public education cannot remain a topic that so few want to deal with.

US students and their futures depend on dealing with the long-standing negative influence of state funding systems on public education. Equity and adequacy are stolen from too many US classrooms. Robbery this brazen cannot be allowed to continue.

Jeff Swensson
Lynn Lehman
John Ellis
Summer 2020

Introduction

Theft in US public education classrooms is a function of funding. Ostensibly provided to maximize the learning of all US students, school funding formulas enacted by state legislatures steal opportunity and adequacy from students and the educators who serve them.

The first chapter of this book lays the groundwork for understanding funding formulas. The basics of school funding in chapter 1 provide readers with the concepts that underlie state funding formulas. These funding systems generate about 90 percent of the funding for public education. Chapter 2 applies this information and introduces readers to the "grab bag" metaphor that represents the workings of funding formulas.

Chapter 3 provides readers with a case study. Because all fifty states have the obligation and responsibility to enact public education, but none are obliged to mirror any specific implementation of another state's responsibility, this case study and the examples provided throughout this book represent the nation's hodgepodge of funding systems.

Chapter 4 explores what school funding pays for. This discussion reveals the *educational gerrymandering, purchasing power,* and *cost versus investment* attributes that contribute to the disarray and disconnection fostered by funding formulas. Chapter 5 asks "are we really paying for what we get?" and details the baleful influence of *productivity* and *bargain-basement dollars* in multiple answers to this question.

Chapters 6 and 7 include insights about the test that education constitutes for any society and how the "magic" of funding for education leads to significant consequences for students, educators, and US society. These chapters speak not only to the extent to which funding promotes a failing grade on the test of education but also the extent to which a looming consequence of the "magic" of contemporary funding for education is *permanence of impermanence.*

Identifying the thief in the classroom is the purpose of chapter 8. Three easy lessons illustrate how legislatures allow this culprit to rob students and educators. This chapter introduces the *funding degradation zone* and its effects.

Chapter 9 seeks a "bottom line" for school funding. This examination reveals only disconnection and misdirection at the bottom line because, in large measure, what is assumed to be the bottom line for school funding is incomplete. Chapter 10 brings this book to its conclusion with a discussion of the evidence that leads to an indictment of school funding.

Chapter One

Dollars and Sense

The Basics of Public School Funding for Educational Programs

A reasonable assumption is that most people would rather have a root canal or stub their toe than delve into the world of public school funding. Despite general disinterest in and avoidance of the topic of school funding, "public education has always been associated with, and more or less dependent on, the solution of problems of adequate school support" (Mort and Ruesser, 1951, p. 3).

State and local taxation are the sources most often tapped to provide school support. Whether the fiscal support for public education generated by these sources is adequate, however, is a serious problem waiting for resolution. A creature left to the processes endemic to the legislature in each state, funding for US public education is described as an unsettled world, a hodgepodge of systems, processes, mechanisms, and outcomes (Born, 2020).

There are occasions when this unsettled world becomes a hot topic. For instance, when state legislators debate the amount of funding that public schools should receive, the public's interest tends to increase. Under these circumstances policymakers and educators wrangle over the system for determining the revenue that will be allocated from the state to school districts. The intensity devoted to these discussions increases when legislators also attend to funding for privatization education (e.g., charter schools, vouchers, tax credits).

The purpose of this chapter is to introduce several basic concepts at the foundation of public school funding. As boredom-inducing as such a purpose may seem, processes that underlie funding for public education shed an intense light on both the serious problems and the remarkable possibilities that afflict and elude US public schools.

Fundamental to an educational system that engages all students with dynamic instruction, reliable leadership, and meaningful outcomes is an

understanding of how public schools are funded. This understanding demands grappling with the equity and adequacy of the appropriation of public
school funds.

To share a baseline for the dollars and sense that establish financial support
for public education, this chapter explores:

- Taxes that generate revenue for schools.
- Sources from which tax revenues are distributed.
- Foundation formulas at the baseline of state support for public schools.
- Cracks in state foundations for public education.
- School funding as input, output, equity, sufficiency, equality, and adequacy.

THE TAX MAN COMETH

Revenue that fulfills the responsibilities and obligations of government is created through taxation. Collecting and distributing tax revenue is fundamental
to one of these responsibilities—traditional public education. And fundamental to understanding traditional public education is an overview of revenue
sources and the taxes derived from them.

Preliminary to an understanding of school finance is the vocabulary associated with revenue for public schools. Several basic terms introduce the
complexity of the relationship between US public education and taxation:

- *Tax base:* The tax base of a locality, school district, or state is the total
  value of taxable income, goods, services, transactions and retail sales,
  property, or other designated items from which governmental entities can
  raise funding.
- *Funding sources:* Three sources of funding—local, state, and federal—
  support US public education. These sources generate revenue for K–12
  public education from taxes that during the 2015–2016 school year, "totaled $706 billion in constant 2017–18 dollars" (McFarland et al., 2019,
  p. 136).
- *Tax rate:* Tax rates are assigned to the various items in the tax base. Often
  indicated as a percentage of the value of taxable items, the tax rate is used
  to calculate the tax yield.
- *Tax yield:* Revenue raised from a tax is referred to as the tax yield.
- *Tax elasticity:* "Elasticity refers to the change in revenue based on a change
  in market conditions or tax rates" (Knoeppel, Pitts, and Lindle, 2013,
  "Policy Coherence," para. 3).

- *Funding level:* A funding level is derived from the combined revenue generated by state and local sources; a funding level does not include any federal revenue for public education.
- *Per-pupil funding level:* The per-pupil funding level for public education in each state is calculated when "state and local revenue [are] divided by student enrollment" (Farrie, Kim, and Sciarra, 2019, p. 2). Funding levels across the United States range from a high of $27,588 in Vermont to a low of $8,569 in Arizona (Farrie et al., 2019, p. 4).
- *Funding distribution:* This term is used to describe the degree or extent of the distribution of categorical, "weighted," or additional funds for school districts with high poverty levels. For example, high-poverty districts in Minnesota receive a per-pupil distribution of $16,434 and low-poverty districts' per-pupil distribution is $12,905 (Farrie et al., 2019, p. 7).
- *Funding effort:* Funding effort is "the level of investment in K–12 public education as a percentage of state wealth (GDP) allocated to maintain and support the state school system" (Farrie et al., 2019, p. 1). Individual school districts also have a wealth factor or *capacity* that may be accessed to augment state financial support.

Within this vocabulary lies the complex, confusing, and often counterproductive state of affairs that typifies local, state, and federal support for US public education.

A Trio of Funding Sources

Three funding sources contribute different amounts to the national total of public school revenue: $58 billion are from the *federal government* (8 percent of the total); $332 billion are derived from *state sources* (47 percent of the total); and the remainder, $316 billion (45 percent of the total), come from *local sources* based on 2017 data (McFarland et al., 2019).

The ratio of support among these three sources changed little one year later during the 2018–2019 school year: 47 percent from state sources, 44.8 percent from local sources, and 8.3 percent from the federal government (Skinner, 2019).

Local Funding and Property Taxes

For the most part, property taxes are the source of local funding for public education (Skinner, 2019). Property taxes can "include a tax on land, tax on the improvements to the land, and a tax on personal property" (Knoeppel et al., 2013, "Policy Coherence," para. 7). Across the nation during the 2015–2016 school year, for instance, 81 percent of the local funding for public schools, around $257 billion, came from property taxes (McFarland et al., 2019).

Property taxes are generally viewed as a stable source of revenue for public schools but "reliance on this source of funding results in uneven tax rates, inconsistent revenues per pupil, and variance in spending across districts" (McGuire and Papke, 2008, as cited in Knoeppel et al., 2013, "Using Educational Research," para. 1). Wildly different revenue amounts are generated from property taxes because "localities in many states are able to select their local property tax rate, at least within a limited range, and may choose to tax themselves at higher rates than other localities in the same state" (Skinner, 2019, p. 5).

Local funding amounts are generated for schools when a tax rate is approved and applied to the assessed valuation of property throughout a school district. Although there are often large funding level differences between districts (Combs, Foster, and Toma, 2018), there are numerous individual school districts with little or no capacity to raise the funding needed when state contributions to public schools leave a gap for local sources to fill.

State Funding from a Variety of Taxes

All state constitutions stipulate that state legislatures have a level of responsibility for the support and maintenance of public education (Knoeppel et al., 2013). "Each state uses a *formula* to distribute state funds to districts. These formulas generally try to account for anticipated differences in the funding capacity between districts" (Weathers and Sosina, 2019, p. 9).

The way that each state approaches a formula varies, and these distribution mechanisms are known by different names such as *foundation formula* or *school finance system*. Foundation formulas are also referred to as *state aid* or as a *foundation grant*.

"The concept of the 'foundation' program is that of establishing an equitable fiscal partnership between the state as a whole and the individual school system charged with the responsibility and privilege of operating the public schools" (Mort and Ruesser, 1951, p. 382). *Foundation formulas*, programs, or systems provide revenue from the state to *local educational agencies* (LEAs) "categorized into five types: (1) Foundation Programs, (2) Full State Funding Programs, (3) Flat Grants, (4) District Power Equalizing, and (5) Categorical Grants" (Skinner, 2019, p. i).

To augment funding raised by taxes, states frequently make some provision in school finance systems to mandate some level of revenue to be generated by local taxation. State foundation programs can specify "at least a minimum rate at which localities must tax themselves . . . [or] . . . a local tax rate is assumed in the calculation of the Foundation Program's state share" (Skinner, 2019, p. 7).

The State of State Taxes

A variety of state taxes generate revenue to support public education: sales tax, personal and corporate income tax, alcoholic beverage tax (one example of an *excise tax*), or capital gains tax (Skinner, 2019). Data from 2019 reveals a nationwide total of $261 billion in revenue from gaming (e.g., lotteries, casinos) that some states also incorporate to fund public education and, thereby, reduce taxes.

When states adopt sales taxes as the primary source of school funding, public education is forced to rely on a volatile revenue stream (Knoeppel et al., 2013). Sales taxes are *elastic* in the sense that the revenue raised depends on economic fluctuations unrelated to the intentions of a foundation formula or the needs of public schools.

Federal Funding

"The federal government's role in public education finance is primarily compensatory" (Weathers and Sosina, 2019, p. 10). Federal funding provides compensatory support to school districts with high concentrations of students in poverty through Elementary and Secondary Education Act (ESEA) Title I, Part A and additional support through Individuals with Disabilities Education Act (IDEA) for students with disabilities (Skinner, 2019). Generally, the amount of this support is linked to the number of students enrolled in district schools who are identified in these categories.

THE SIMILARITIES OF SCHOOL FUNDING

Because public education is not mentioned in the US Constitution and, therefore, is a power reserved to the states, each legislature responds to language in its state constitution with schemes to support public schools. Nuances, variations, eccentricities, and labyrinths emerge as a result from the fifty legislatures to guide the aggregation and allocation of funding for public education. Although foundation formulas in the states vary, there are similarities for accruing tax dollars to fund public schools.

The *foundation grant* is primary among these similarities. In theory, these legislature-designed calculations ensure that "every district receives the same amount of per-pupil funding because it is assumed that all students are the same" (Johnson and Vesely, 2017, p. 92). Skinner (2019) describes foundation formulas as a state's per-pupil funding "target." As such, these grants are a minimum level of funding believed to be "necessary to provide an 'adequate' educational program" (Skinner, 2019, p. 6).

A foundation formula, grant, or program is the baseline of funding for public education in four out of every five states (Skinner, 2019).

A foundation program is the use of a formula to determine how much money a school district will need to operate, then it determines what percentage of that need will be funded by the state and what will be required of the local systems to contribute to the need (Larkin, 2016, p. 17).

The impact of foundation formulas has grown over time because states have taken on more of the funding for education to move away from reliance on local contributions from property taxes (Knoeppel et al., 2013; Skinner, 2019). Scholars document a deep-seated resentment toward property taxes sometimes expressed in "class action suits brought in state supreme courts that challenged the finance systems in the respective states" (Knoeppel et al., 2013, "Policy Coherence," para. 6).

The Similarity of Funding Inequity

The needs of different students, the capacities of different school districts to raise revenue, the demand to decrease property taxes, and numerous court challenges are harbingers of the numerous difficulties associated with equity of funding. Put simply, these are indicators that the standard amounts of per-pupil funding from state foundation formulas do not provide equal access and opportunity for all students. State funding systems often are similarly inequitable.

Given the damage to teaching and learning that lurks in this similarity and given that the ostensible purpose of a foundation program is to equalize funding on a per-pupil basis throughout public schools in a state, legislators explore various means to establish more equal foundation grants.

To this end, some funding programs incorporate more funding for high-need student cohorts (e.g., English-language learners, low income, special education). If a state's foundation funding does not include this additional revenue, separate Categorical Grants may "provide increased funds to serve specific high-need pupil groups" (Skinner, 2019, p. 9).

Categorical grants are established by thirty-two states to "weight" different high-need student cohorts with different dollar amounts and, in the case of students with special needs, "higher weights are assigned as the level of disability increases" (Skinner, 2019, p 11).

Similar Cracks in the Funding Foundation

Foundation amounts provide revenue "only up to a target level, with LEAs often free to raise additional funds (not matched by the state) if they wish" (Skinner, 2019, p. 7). This funding reality entails disparities that arise when LEAs can, or cannot, raise additional funding. Moreover, categorical funding (either within the foundation grant or from categorical grants) usually does not provide sufficient revenue to meet identified student needs (Morgan and Amerikaner, 2018).

Sufficient revenue, equitable revenue, adequate revenue, fair revenue—all represent cracks in the foundation of public school funding. The fragmentation that afflicts school funding, as Brimley, Verstegan, and Garfield (2012) point out, accelerates because "equity should not be considered synonymous with *equality* in this context. Equality means treating everyone the same. Equity means treating them fairly" (p. 50). Equity from a foundation formula is not a unifying fiscal outcome. Instead, equity constitutes a proverbial fork-in-the-funding-road.

One way equity "splits" is when it is considered as a construct that is either *vertical* or *horizontal* (Baker and Corcoran, 2012). Another way that equity "splits" is when it is considered as a matter that applies either to students or to taxpayers. A third "split" develops when school funding is either *equitable* or *adequate.*

Upside Down or Right Side up? Horizontal or Vertical Equity?

Horizontal equity refers to "equal funding on behalf of similar pupils in different LEAs across a state" (Skinner, 2019, p. 9). Horizontal equity describes the traditional understanding of a foundation formula that provides a system for equitable funding under which "all students would have access to a similar amount, or 'package' or resources" (Ladd, 2008, p. 404, as cited in Knoeppel et al., 2013, "Competing Priorities," para. 2).

Vertical equity, on the other hand, describes varied levels of funding allocated based on students' different levels of need. Vertical equity posits funding that accounts for differentially situated schools, differential treatment of students with different needs, and the requirement for more or different resources to establish equitable outcomes (Knoeppel et al., 2013).

Equity for Whom: Students or Taxpayers?

"For students, equity may be defined as 'equality of educational opportunity or equality of access to educational opportunities'" (Johnson and Vesely, 2017, p. 92). The extent to which funding distribution manifests equity for all students in public schools is an enduring concern.

This concern is raised persistently because legislators and policymakers attempt to balance equitable revenue to meet the needs of students with equitable taxation to meet the needs and concerns of taxpayers (Knoeppel et al., 2013).

School funding becomes a balancing act when "states are also concerned with equitable treatment of taxpayers, as ultimately taxpayers bear the burden of financing education" (Johnson and Vesely, 2017, p. 93). What's fair? For whom? These questions linger during any consideration of foundation formulas and revenue for public schools.

Equity or Adequacy?

Vocabulary and concepts at the foundation of funding for US public schools only hint at enduring with equity and adequacy embedded in state funding formulas (Knoeppel et al., 2013). Moreover, as scholars observe, "simply offering equal funding isn't enough" (Morgan and Amerikaner, 2018, p. 3).

This means not only that a state's offer or intention to provide equal funding doesn't come to pass often but also that whatever revenue develops for a school district from foundation formulas frequently is inadequate to the task of providing an education sufficient to meet the needs of all students.

A CRUMBLING FOUNDATION

There is a difference between expenditures of a school district and the amount of revenue allocated to the district by the state's foundation grant. Part of this difference is explained by the economic premise that "wants" are always unlimited, while "resources" are always limited. A different explanation for this reality lies in the extent of the societal or political willingness to tax in support of public education.

Put bluntly, state constitutions mandate a requirement to support public education for all students but state legislatures respond to this task with varying interpretations of the funding required to enact the expectations in vague constitutional language about public schooling.

Historically, fiscal support for "all students" in public schools has been limited. Funding first ignored students with special needs. Although the early history of funding often included revenue for a state school for students with visual or hearing impairments, early funding formulas infrequently provided categorical support to school districts for students with disabilities.

History also provides ample evidence of funding at higher levels for districts with predominantly White enrollment while districts serving students of color are allocated less revenue (Black, 2019).

The gaps created by these enduring characteristics of public education—rooted in the chasm between constitutional implications for state support of public education and the legislative reluctance to fund seemingly noble intentions—widen when legislatures decide the value of teaching and learning within their annual budgets. "Some states in their budgets fail to provide the amount of state revenue or 'aid' required by the states own funding formula, a condition called 'formula underfunding'" (Farrie et al., 2019, p. 2).

Equal access and equal opportunity, under circumstances like these, are promises rarely delivered fairly by foundation formulas. The enduring conundrum associated with funding for public education cannot be avoided: Is funding for public education a *cost* or an *investment*?

IS SCHOOL FUNDING FAIR?
IS SCHOOL FUNDING SUFFICIENT?

Asking whether school funding can be fair or sufficient often yields two questions in response: fair to whom and sufficient for what? Conventional wisdom about public education supplies two pat answers: *to students* and *for learning*.

Obvious answers to critical questions, however, hide the practical and ideological conflicts that fragment fiscal support for public education. Tax rates, funding level, funding distribution, and funding effort are matters over which disagreement, disparity, and division reign and within which fairness and sufficiency are uncertain propositions.

Choices for Fair Funding: Regressive, Flat, or Progressive

Most states generate support for public schools that is either *regressive* or *flat*. Flat funding for public education (in seventeen states) means "there is no appreciable increase in funding to address the need for additional resources in high-poverty districts" (Farrie et al., 2019, p. 8).

Regressive funding occurs in fifteen states that distribute more revenue to low-poverty school districts than to high-poverty districts. For instance, low-poverty districts in Illinois generate an average per-pupil funding of $17,028, but high-poverty districts average per-pupil distribution is $12,530 (Farrie et al., 2019, p. 7).

Seventeen of the remaining states provide a *progressive* distribution system. This happens when a state allocates more funding to high-poverty school districts than to low-poverty districts (Farrie et al., 2019, p. 8). (*Authors' note:* One state, Hawaii, is unaccounted for in research about funding distribution because the entire state is one school district. That means no revenue comparisons between different school districts are possible.)

Funding level and distribution are keys to the extent to which any state's revenue for public education is fair and sufficient. Whether the funds allocated to a school district are sufficient to meet the tasks and goals expected of public schools, however, does not necessarily correspond to a state's funding level.

An example from Connecticut illustrates this point: "although Connecticut's funding level is $4,954 per pupil above the national average, the state provides, on average, 15% less funding to high-poverty districts than to low-poverty districts" (Farrie et al., 2019, p. 6).

Choosing Sufficient Funding

There is little agreement about the amount of funding that is sufficient to support public education. Ignoring, for a moment, the funding level disparities between individual school districts and the funding targets missed by state budgets, sufficient funding for public education appears to have an elasticity of its own depending on the student outcomes deemed appropriate and desirable at any given time in US history.

When US public schools first were created during the agricultural era of the 1800s, the outcomes most students required were minimally academic. Appropriate and desirable for the twenty-first century, however, are student outcomes that have evolved to become critical skills. "Critical skills of the future will be those that allow students to adapt, learn new tasks and become productive in a highly automated environment" (Hicks, 2019, n.p.), a vast composite set of cognitive, creative, and behavioral capabilities that other scholars have referred to as *how to think* (Swensson and Shaffer, 2020).

To be fair and sufficient for the remainder of the twenty-first century, funding allocated by state legislatures to public schools requires an expanded and encompassing baseline with an elasticity of its own.

The Inputs and Outputs of Public School Funding

Until relatively recently, the impact of revenue for public education was understood as an *input* and the extent to which this input was equitable involved discussion about the *fairness* and *sufficiency* of public school funding.

However, as Johnson and Vesely (2017) observe, "equity and equality are not always the same. The pursuit of equitable treatment often results in the unequal distribution of resources" (p. 92). As illustrated previously, foundation formulas that establish horizontal equity are not capable of the more robust funding support for students established when foundation programs evince vertical equity.

School funding that yields equity and sufficiency has been challenged by the advent of free market theory and its emphasis on efficiency as the premiere baseline for US public education. Knoeppel et al. (2013) summarize this challenge: "Economists define efficiency as the allocation of inputs to achieve maximum levels of outputs . . . [and define inefficiency] . . . in schools where costs exceed outputs" ("Discussion," para. 2). For proponents of free market schooling (often referred to as *choice education* or *privatization education*) outputs are preferred as the primary measure of the efficiency of state funding for schools.

How to judge revenue for public schools that entails fairness or sufficiency has changed over time. Lawsuits challenged school funding as an input. The result of numerous such cases is that state funding for public education "has evolved from a focus on equity, defined as equal, to one of adequacy, defined as sufficient" (Ladd, 2008; Darling-Hammond & Snyder, 2003; Verstegen, 2002; Reschovsky & Imazeki, 2001, as cited in Knoeppel et al., 2013, "Using Educational Research," para. 2).

CAN FUNDING FOR US PUBLIC EDUCATION BE ADEQUATE?

Every concept, mechanism, process, and formula associated with state funding for public education can be considered in relation to one basic idea: adequacy. But state legislators are at a disadvantage when it comes to determining adequate funding for public education.

In the first place, few legislators have ever been public educators. Next, few state legislators visit public schools when they are in session or convene advisory groups of constituents who do serve in public schools. Finally, state legislators tend to rely on proximal ideologies to guide their decision-making about public school finance.

Lack of experience in and with public education alongside ideologically affirming perspectives infuse the decisions of legislators about public school finance.

Combined, a knowledge gap, an experience vacuum, and a tendency to gravitate to ideological solutions attached to personally validating allegiances yield a crazy quilt of legislative decisions about public school funding across the United States. Adequacy of funding and the perception of an adequate education, as a result, are affixed to one outcome that any legislator can relate to: testing.

As the third decade of the twenty-first century unfolds, the output of first resort used to judge the adequacy of funding, and all other aspects of public education, is standardized testing. On a parallel course with testing trending as adequacy in public schools is a chorus of voices demanding the reduction of property taxes. "The public continues to express resentment toward this tax and politically empowered groups whittle it away through demand for exemption or other favored treatment" (Kent & Sowards, 2009, as cited in Knoeppel et al., 2013, "Policy Coherence," para. 6).

Under the influence of testing, free market theory, efficiency, and taxpayer angst, the notion of adequacy of public education is reduced to an expression of minimums (Swensson and Shaffer, 2020). Farrie et al. (2019) offer a blunt characterization of the ultimate minimum embedded in funding for US public education when they observe that "in many states and high poverty districts, public schools are severely and chronically underfunded" (p. 2).

This doleful state of affairs throughout US public education teaching and learning represents the elasticity associated with underfunding. State legislatures undergo significant contortions to meet constitutional imperatives to support public schools while evading a focus on the educational necessities for all students during the twenty-first century.

It is in the fiscal gymnastics performed by state legislators where a carnival-like approach to public education develops: Adequacy becomes a matter of laughable minimums, and equity becomes a forgotten educational imperative.

Chapter Two

Grab Bag Funding

Promises, Problems, and Prizes

School carnivals feature a variety of booths where games and diversions—tossing a ping pong ball to win a goldfish swimming in a small bowl, anyone?—offer family fun to raise funds. Frequently, one of these booths offers a grab bag. For the price of a ticket, an event-goer reaches into a bag to grab a simple toy as a prize to take home.

This carnival booth and state systems for public school funding are alike. They begin with the unknown, what cannot be seen within the grab bag. As scholars observe, school funding formulas offer massive grab bags filled with unknowns: "except for a handful of experts and legislative staff, no one understands what the state is doing or its real-world impact on students" (Black, 2019, p. 1395).

Filled with mystery and laden with complexity, school funding grab bags are just as likely to yield problems or promises as they are prizes. Cubberley (1905), in the early days of the twentieth century, described this reality: "one of the most important administrative problems of today is how properly to finance the school system of a state, as the question of sufficient revenue lies back of almost every other problem" (p. 3).

This reality is just as relevant in the twenty-first century as scholars equate a school district's budget with the district's educational plan (Coffin and Cooper, 2016). However, there is no one-size-fits all description of programs and formulas for school funding because each state cobbles together its own system or formula to determine funding level, effort, and distribution.

In this chapter, problems, promises, and prizes pulled out of funding system grab bags emerge as representative examples of a struggle to establish equitable and adequate revenue for all public schools. State legislatures, state courts, state leaders, and policymakers all play a role in the creation and interpretation of each representation of funding for public education.

The purpose of this chapter is to shed light on funding systems for public education. This exploration will incorporate issues galvanized to public school finance including equity, sufficiency, adequacy, and justice. State court determinations related to these issues and the response of legislatures to court findings will also be shared.

The grab bag approach to funding US public education yields an assortment of prizes and problems that exist because a promise underlies the reach for revenue for public education.

THE PROMISE IN THE SCHOOL FUNDING
GRAB BAG: "BETTER"

Between 80 and 90 percent of the spending by any US school district pays for educators and staff who establish, sustain, and grow learning experiences and achievement for US students. Every school funding formula supports these professionals and the instruction that leads to academic engagement for students.

Although it is important to remember that the fifty different funding programs also allocate revenue to support transportation, construction, debt service, building maintenance, technology, and utilities/insurance, the primary intention of revenue for schools—and the focus of the discussion throughout this book—is to provide for high-quality teaching and learning.

The funding level, effort, and distribution undertaken by a state are directed toward two major perspectives about education and instruction: (i) traditional public education and (ii) privatization or choice education (e.g., charter schools, virtual schools, vouchers). Privatization education arises from a free market perspective that envisions, for instance, charter schools as learning environments that "trade traditional oversight and regulation mechanisms, like democratically elected school boards, for stricter accountability for student outcomes and the added burden of competing in the education market" (Naclerio, 2017, p. 1161).

These two major perspectives are the first of many choices that lie before legislators and policymakers when decisions are made about foundation formulas. These decisions allocate funding to serve the almost 77 million US students enrolled in traditional public schools as of the 2017–2018 school year and the 3.2 million students enrolled in charter schools (Gilblom and Sang, 2019).

Education: Its Promise and the Problem of Funding

The promise of education is "better." Better individual capacities, a better life, a better job, a better community, a better future, a better society—all and more are the opportunities at the core of education's promise. In the United States, this "better" also includes a better democracy and a better engagement in democracy by well-educated citizens.

From both major perspectives about education in the United States, there is agreement that education is a necessary societal function. Proponents of both perspectives reach into the funding grab bag intending to grasp different visions of "better." Advocates of these perspectives also concur that funding from local, state, federal, or private sources is essential to better schooling (Baker and Corcoran, 2012). Reaching into the funding grab bag is the means to fulfill the promises of "better."

The promise of education is forestalled, however, by significant problems associated with school funding. As described by Morgan and Amerikaner (2018), it turns out that funding is an enduring obstacle to "better:"

> The educational opportunities provided to the nearly 51 million children who attend public schools are anything but equal. Students of different races, ethnicities, and socioeconomic backgrounds tend to end up at very different schools, ones with disparate resources, including those most crucial to student success— for example, high quality teachers, [and an] effective early education program (p. 3).

Apparent agreement by the two major perspectives that schooling is a necessity, or that education leads to "better," or that public funding sources are required, does not arise from agreement about the purpose and funding of public education.

How Best to Fund "Better"

The worth of education and the funding that supports it can be accounted for by three factors: that education occupies center stage "in modern societies and the myriad opportunities it affords; the scarcity of high-quality educational opportunities for many children; and the critical role of the state in providing educational opportunities. These factors differentiate education from many other social goods" (Shields, Newman, and Satz, 2017, "The Scarcity," para. 1).

How each perspective about education—traditional public education and privatization education—applies funding from the grab bag to fund the worth of education exposes two separate versions of "better" for US education.

A HISTORY LESSON: FUNDAMENTAL CHARACTERISTICS
OF US PUBLIC EDUCATION

Jung (2018) observes that "two conditions should be met in order for a product or service to be a public good: non-excludable and non-rival" (Varian 2010; Samuelson 1954, as cited on p. 100).

Simply put, the distinguishing characteristic of a public good like traditional US public education is that it must be available to everyone whether they pay taxes or not (nonexcludable) and that one individual's use of or involvement with this public good cannot prevent any other person from the same use or involvement (nonrival).

As a public good, US public education reflects and responds to societal, cultural, personal, economic, and other factors that influence the lives and the learning of students. The promise offered by traditional public education since its inception in the 1830s is fueled by teachers and staff members dedicated to something greater than themselves.

"In the first half of the 20th century, public education in the United States was highly decentralized, with local governments providing an average of 80% or more of all revenues for public elementary and secondary schools" (Corcoran, Romer, and Rosenthal, 2017, p. 1).

Nonexcludable and nonrival, US public education manifests a public good in the service of public educators (including teachers, counselors, social workers, nurses, librarians, school resource officers, support personnel, and school leaders) who teach and guide the nation's students.

The public good, furthermore, is represented by all students (some of whom are affected by mental health issues, substance abuse issues, violence, bullying, depression, poverty, or family disruption) engaged in learning by traditional public educators. The instruction and learning at the core of traditional public education reflects an investment "in additional specialized pupil support services personnel [who] can address student needs that interfere with learning" (Partelow, Shapiro, McDaniels, and Brown, 2018, "Lack of Funding," para. 3).

Finally, a distinguishing characteristic of traditional public education is its reciprocal relationship with US democracy. Citizenship in a democracy requires an inclusive give-and-take that can only be achieved if an educated populace accords to each person nonexcludable and nonrival rights. Citizenship education—historically, a primary purpose of public education (Swensson, Ellis, and Shaffer, 2019a)—supports the exercise of democracy and requires funding from the public sources established in democracy.

In the Present Day: History and Promise

The promise of public education that evinces the common good as nonexcludable and nonrival is not understood in the same way by advocates of the two major perspectives about US education. Although proponents of quality education for students in the United States speak to the general value, from both points of view, of schooling committed to "better," congruence about the promise of education and the funding that creates it goes no further.

These two perspectives about "better" from US public education exemplify what scholars refer to as *preference substitution*. "Preference substitution occurs when different institutions or actors in a market for public goods or services value different dimensions of that good or service—when they define 'quality' differently" (Carlson, Cowen, and Fleming, 2013, p. 902).

Differing perspectives about "better" in US education lead, inevitably, to the different funding ideologies and visions that afflict funding systems for education throughout the United States.

FROM SEA TO SHINING SEA: STATE FUNDING SYSTEMS

Foundation formulas or grants establish per-pupil funding for school districts. The revenue provided to local districts from states covers instructional program "costs such as general formula assistance, special education, bilingual education, gifted and talented programs, employee benefits, capital outlay, vocational education programs, and staff improvement programs" (Weathers and Sosina, 2019, p. 9). "A number of studies have found that greater spending on instruction, especially the quality of teachers, tends to provide stronger leverage on student achievement than many other uses of funds" (Darling-Hammond, 2019, p. 7).

Representative Examples of State Funding for Education

State funding systems are the wellspring for teaching and learning in public education. Funding level and funding distribution have an impact on educators' salaries, teacher-to-pupil ratios, support services for students, the length of a school day and year, along with other factors that affect the quality of teaching and learning. Several states represent the impact of funding on the instructional mission of public schools:

- *In Missouri:* The share of state aid provided to school districts (41 percent of district revenue) is less than the national average but a foundation formula revised in the early 2000s is "driven by setting a foundation target with student-need adjustments (S.B. 287)" (Baker and Corcoran, 2012, p. 17).

- *In Pennsylvania:* A foundation system that "adopted new student-need and cost adjustments" was promulgated in 2008 and designed "to be phased in over the next several years but has since been dismantled" (Baker and Corcoran, 2012, p. 18).
- *In Texas:* The school finance system was found to be unconstitutional because, as the state court determined, it forced school districts to levy a maximum property tax rate that constituted a statewide property tax (Baker and Corcoran, 2012).
- *In North Carolina:* State aid for education "appears to vary little with respect to differing poverty rates across counties. The lowest-poverty county districts appear to receive nearly as much state aid per pupil as the highest-poverty counties" (Baker and Corcoran, 2012, p. 19).
- *In Indiana:* Revenue from the state to school districts "is calculated using the per-pupil amount multiplied by the district's total student enrollment (or average daily membership [ADM]); additional funding is calculated through a complexity formula that takes into account the socioeconomic level of each district's students" (Moon and Stewart, 2016, p. 3).

State Funding for Traditional Public Education

Property taxes constituted the primary source of funding for K–12 public education in most states before the 1970s (Jackson, Johnson, and Persico, 2016). Under these circumstances, revenue disparities were built in. Even after funding formulas began to reverse course and incorporate larger contributions from state taxation, equitable funding remained elusive. For instance, the average annual per-pupil expenditures in fiscal year 2013 ranged from $17,982 in New Jersey to $6,312 in Utah (National Center for Education Statistics [NCES], n.d.).

State Funding for Privatization Education

A web of statutes, legislative interventions, third-party providers, and funding mechanisms facilitate state attention to privatization education. Vouchers, charter schools, and educational savings accounts are among the mechanisms that require state funding or funding facilitated by state statute on behalf of privatization schooling. Funding from the state for privatization or choice education is engineered several different ways.

Often, the per-pupil amount allocated for traditional public schools "follows" a student to a charter school where the student enrolls. State funding for vouchers, in states such as Louisiana, Arizona, Indiana, and Wisconsin, is provided "completely through the state general funds" (Stewart and Moon, 2016a, p. 6). Education savings accounts are contributions to privatization education from individuals or businesses that reduce the tax liability owed to the state.

These free market–based approaches to education intend competition in a marketplace under the assumption that this creates an increase in school quality and saves "public funds if a voucher costs less than the per-pupil funding amount" (Spalding, 2014, as cited in Stewart and Moon, 2016a, p. 1).

Proponents of choice education, nevertheless, complain about less to spend when, for example, "charter-school students across 30 states and the District of Columbia on average received $3,814 less in funding than TPS students, a funding gap of 28.4 percent" (Wolf et al., 2014, p. 8).

ACCOUNTABILITY: MISSING FROM THE GRAB BAG

Accountability for funding of US education is too often taken for granted. Because public revenue is acquired and allocated for both traditional public education and privatization education, keeping track of this funding seems like a straightforward and necessary accounting.

Accountability for funding, however, is a responsibility understood differently by educational advocates, legislators, ideologues, and policymakers. Privatization education proponents promote *outcome accountability*, while traditional public educators embrace *operational accountability* (Naclerio, 2017).

Outcome accountability is a focus on outputs to the detriment of accountability for throughput (Swensson and Shaffer, 2020). Operational accountability, conversely, is a focus on procedures, practices, and professional choices that embraces oversight and continuous improvement (Naclerio, 2017; Swensson, Ellis, and Shaffer, 2019b).

Split in two, accountability becomes another of the dualities that infest education and its funding. Fragmentation, once again, shatters education as a public good when, as will be discussed, accountability devolves into the pretense that simple addition is the outcome that justifies theft in the classroom. Moreover, accountability can be impossible when "financial reporting on charter schools is often inconsistent, incomplete regarding revenue sources and expenditures, and imprecise regarding specifics of resource allocation" (Baker, Libby, and Wiley, 2012, p. 1).

STATE LEGISLATURES AND
THE BASICS OF SCHOOL FUNDING

State legislatures embrace, to one degree or another, the responsibility for funding public education derived from language in each state's constitution. The constitutions of Florida and Illinois, for example, speak to a requirement for high-quality education while, in New York, the constitution speaks only to maintaining free common schools (Atchison, 2019, p. 3).

Responding to varied, sometimes vague, constitutional language, state legislatures enact funding for public education without paying attention to equal funding allocated for all school districts (Atchison, 2019; Baker, 2014).

Equity is a term used to describe "the extent to which states allocate funding so that low-wealth districts . . . and students with greater needs get more, so that they can reach an adequate level of educational opportunities and outcomes" (Darling-Hammond, 2019, p. 4). Any attempt to address equity in school funding, however, comes face-to-face with a paradox.

The gist of this paradox is conveyed in the basics of school funding. To establish equity, a state's funding level must generate sufficient dollars to accommodate the cost of educating all students in any district. Funding allocation, therefore, will be unequal between districts. Low-wealth districts, districts with higher proportions of special needs students, or districts welcoming more English-language learners will be supported with more revenue from the state's funding system to realize statewide equity.

To this end, it is important to remember that "'Cost' and 'spending' are not the same. Cost refers to the minimum amount that must be spent to achieve any particular outcome goal, whereas spending is merely what was spent, regardless of outcomes" (Baker et al., 2012, p. 6). Cost, in this sense, is sometimes mistaken as adequacy and adequacy is frequently invoked as minimum funding.

Public Money Under Private Management

Public funding for education in the United States extends into private management for schools through a variety of mechanisms (e.g., charter schools, vouchers, tax-credit "scholarships") associated with free market theory (Swensson et al., 2019a).

One way this takes shape is through "state charter school laws [that] allow private companies and firms to take part in competitive education markets in the attempt to depart from a 'one-size-fits-all' model" (Miron, Evergreen, and Urschel, 2008; Scott and DiMartino, 2010, as cited in Lee, 2018, p. 3). Educational management organizations (EMOs) operate many privatization schools and, often, on a for-profit basis. EMOs are third-party entities bal-lyhooed for their intent to dissolve the one-size-fits-all nature of traditional public education.

When public money is allocated to third-party entities, the negative impact on traditional school districts can be devastating. In the Trenton (New Jersey) Public Schools, long-term underfunding by the state alongside rapid increases in the number of charter schools, led to a per-pupil spending reduction of $2,694 between 2008 and 2018 (Farrie, 2018).

When the State Won't, Local Taxation Must

The revenue provided by a state foundation formula to a school district is often an amount that substitutes spending for the funding required for ad-equacy. Local taxation is left to ameliorate this impact. The state's funding level often leaves school districts high and dry, especially in communities without the capacity for a local tax rate that can compensate for the state's funding shortfall.

In some cases, state legislatures choose "not to levy sufficient taxes to support *any* high-quality public services" (Baker, DiCarlo, and Weber, 2019, p. 7). Public education, under these circumstances, faces an uphill climb when states like Arizona or North Carolina have less capacity (e.g., sizeable economies; residents with relatively high incomes) and establish low funding effort "measured in terms of spending as a proportion of capacity" (Baker et al., 2019, p. 7)

As Baker et al. (2019) indicate, funding effort "is in large part a policy choice representing both the decision to levy sufficient taxes and how the state prioritizes public education" (p. 7).

The extent to which a state prioritizes traditional public education can be measured by choices made to allocate revenue to privatization education. Ob-servers of US education illustrated, as the third decade of the twenty-first cen-tury dawned, that "15 states and the District of Columbia now have voucher programs; 18 offer tax-credit scholarships that provide wealthy donors and corporations generous tax breaks for donating to private-school scholarship funds" (Berkshire, 2019, n.p.).

Legislatures and Funding Equity

If the authors of state constitutions hoped that state legislatures would enact equitable school funding, this hope never had a fighting chance.

Equitable funding for all students in any state evaporated swiftly because the bedrock of finance systems for the first century of public education in the

United States was local funding from property taxes (Combs et al., 2018). Until the midpoint of the twentieth century, 80 percent of funding for public education came from local sources (Corcoran et al., 2017; Skinner, 2019).

Equitable school funding, under these circumstances, rarely emerges from funding systems that depend on the widely divergent tax bases of local school districts throughout any state. "Across the country, the highest poverty districts receive about $1,000, or 7 percent, less per pupil in state and local funding than the lowest poverty districts" (Morgan and Amerikaner, 2018, p. 6).

Trending: Local or State Funding Sources?

Reliance on local funding for US public schools, however, is waning. A combination of concern over inequities emerging from dramatically different local funding levels and angst over local property tax rates led to a variety of legislative and judicial interventions that altered dependence on local funding for public schools.

The extent of the trend away from local funding sources is reflected in an overview of the ratio of funding in the second decade of the twenty-first century from the three main sources of school funding: 47 percent is derived from state sources; 44.8 percent is generated from local sources; and federal sources provide 8.3 percent (Skinner, 2019).

Trends, however, do not incorporate the same ratio between funding sources in all states. By way of illustration, in the 2015–2016 school year, more than half of all funding came from state sources in twenty-three states. But "in 15 states and the District of Columbia, at least half of all revenue came from local governments" (McFarland et al., 2019, p. 137). This means that the basics of school funding can contravene equity. Intentions "to reduce variation in spending among districts" (Atchison, 2019, p. 3) are neither envisioned nor realized across all states.

Researchers find, for instance, that states that spend heavily on public education (e.g., Connecticut, Massachusetts, New Jersey, and Vermont) generate as much as three times the funding level of "low-spending states such as Arizona, Nevada, and North Carolina" (Darling-Hammond, 2019, p. 4). In Alabama, this funding conundrum leads to funding "students in high-poverty districts at 90% of what it funds students in low-poverty districts" (Larkin, 2016, p. 17).

In Illinois, 60 percent of the funding generated for public education is provided by local sources and this reflects "the state's policy of over-reliance on local property taxes and insufficient levels of state revenue to fund property-poor, high poverty districts" (Farrie et al., 2019, p. 9).

FUNDING SNAFUS: FROM THE LEGISLATURE
TO THE COURTROOM

As the first century of public school funding from local sources reveals, equity has not been a frequent feature of public school funding systems. Since the 1960s, the struggle to provide equitable funding from a state has been transformed into a focus on adequacy. Integral to this transition are state courts.

Initially, state courts entered the school funding fray to adjudicate cases brought to end revenue disparities between school districts within the same state. "For equity cases, local financing was found to violate the responsibility of the state to provide a quality education to all children" (Jackson et al., 2016, p. 162).

Although court decisions regarding these cases could lead to an "increase in district level funding, more progressive funding patterns, and narrower gaps in expenditures between high- and low-income districts" (Candelaria and Shores 2017; Card and Payne 2002; Jackson et al., 2016; Lafortune et al., 2018, as cited in Weathers and Sosina, 2019, p. 5), adjudication of funding equity led to mixed results.

Funding Litigation Pivots: Equity to Adequacy

Litigation to reform funding of public education pivoted from equity to adequacy. Cases brought concerning the adequacy of school funding usually involve a challenge based on a state's constitutional provision requiring a free and adequate level of education (Jackson et al., 2016). Put another way, adequacy requires that "progressive distributions of funding must be coupled with sufficient overall levels of funding to achieve the desired outcomes" (Baker et al., 2019, p. 5). The pivot to adequacy turns away from adult-centric funding goals and turns toward student-centric funding.

Nothing about this pivot is easy because another view of adequacy has prevailed in various state courts and from the perspective of different legislatures. Ironically, this different understanding holds that minimum education and minimum funding are adequate. This view of adequacy is "defined as a measure of whether the amount of funding for schools is enough for students to reach a minimal level of education outcomes" (Baker et al., 2019, p. 9). The impact of defining *adequate* as a *minimum* in US public education is a never-ending disaster (Swensson and Shaffer, 2020).

The Funding Adequacy Tennis Match

"As of 2018, 22 states have had plaintiff victories in the respective state's highest court indicating an unconstitutional system of funding schools"

(Atchison, 2019, p. 3). But a successful challenge to the adequacy of a funding system can quickly evolve into what amounts to a tennis match between the state courts and legislature. Once a court case is resolved in favor of plaintiffs seeking redress of funding system failure, the legislature has decisions to make about a return volley, a response to the court's findings.

The return volley by legislatures is often a lengthy delay or a distraction. For example, the Supreme Court of the State of North Carolina, in *Leandro v. State*, ordered a "remedy [for] deficiencies in the equity and adequacy of their state school finance system" (Baker and Corcoran, 2012, p. 19). Eight years later, no substantive change had been enacted by the legislature.

Sometimes, state courts respond with deference to the legislature when a funding formula is challenged. The Illinois State Supreme Court, for example, heard *Committee v. Edgar* in which plaintiffs argued that the Illinois foundation formula was neither high quality nor efficient as required in the language of the state's constitution.

The court decided that education is not a right guaranteed under the Illinois constitution. Deference was given to the legislature's responsibility for public education. Thus, the funding formula "was neither unconstitutional nor [was it] within the scope of the Court's authority to evaluate whether it was efficient or high quality" (Fitzgerald, 2015, p. 55).

New Jersey could be the "poster child" for the school funding tennis match featuring judicial action and legislative response. Starting in 1996–1997, and during the ensuing thirty years of volleys between the legislature and the courts consisting of nine rulings from the courts, New Jersey committed to an investment in parity for high-poverty and minority school districts.

By 2007, this substantial dedication to funding for the improvement of instruction led to New Jersey "ranking in the top five states in all subject areas and grade levels on the NAEP" (Darling-Hammond, 2019, p. 15). Adequate funding is not the norm, however, throughout the Garden State. The machinations of state leaders, directed at the Trenton Public Schools (TPS), resulted "in an over $41 million shortfall in state aid to TPS in 2017–18" (Farrie, 2018, p. 1).

Adequacy and "Better"

Across the United States, the turn away from equity and toward the adequacy of funding coincided with the movement to use standardized testing as the best way to measure "better." Numerous scholars describe this as a shift away from inputs and equity to outputs and standardized testing. In this way of thinking, yet another understanding of adequacy emerges. "Adequacy has often been defined as the amount and kind of education needed to allow students to meet those standards" (Atchison, 2019; Darling-Hammond, 2019, p. 4; Farrie et al., 2019).

Adequacy became linked to outcome accountability and the drive to establish adequacy in public education became "better" as it is understood by free market theory. The damaging effect of this linkage between standardized test results and funding adequacy will be discussed later.

A Federal Referee for the Adequacy Tennis Match

Where federal funding and statutes enter the public school classroom, litigation follows. The US Supreme Court (*Board of Education v. Rowley*) determined that free appropriate public education (FAPE) is a requirement that the education accessed by special education students must "'be sufficient to confer some educational benefit'" (Naclerio, 2017, p. 1166).

The nature of sufficiency or adequacy, however, was not stipulated in this decision, and the court posited no test that could be applied to determine adequacy. This decision effectively removed the lines on the imaginary tennis court of funding for public education.

THE INDIVIDUAL GOOD: A GRAB BAG PRIZE

The common good is the prize in the funding grab bag usually associated with traditional public education. From a radically different perspective, however, the individual good is the prize sought from the funding grab bag.

The individual good is the purpose of education from the perspective of privatization adherents. Individuals, in this view, gain competitive advantage from schooling. The function of education is to equip individuals for economic and life success welded to self-aggrandizement for survival of the fittest. One privatization schooling proponent affirms self-aggrandizement as "better" because "education strongly affects the future economic returns that individuals see" (Hanushek, 2020, p. 1).

Low-Cost: The Extended Prize

Free market education not only offers individual good but it also offers low cost as the centerpiece of privatization education. This extended prize coincides with free market theory and its view of education as a cost and not an investment.

Public education is a cost to government and a burden to taxpayers. The prize package sought by advocates of privatization education is schooling that is "(a) more effective and (b) less costly, while (c) serving the same children as regular district schools" (Baker et al., 2012, p. 2). The least funding for an efficient delivery of teaching and learning is "better."

Free market prizes lead policymakers to cost-reduction conclusions tied to schemes in which highly effective teachers are offered "extra pay to accept larger class sizes (a trade-off that many teachers indicate they are willing to take), the higher pay becomes extra pay for extra work—and more students are taught by the best teachers" (Hanushek, 2020, p. 10). Piling on the number of students per classroom allows the elimination of teaching positions to reduce cost, while advantaging individuals seated in Lancasterian-esque learning environments.

Funding for "Better:" I Know a Good School Funding System When I See One

A reputable system for accruing and allocating revenue can be described in several ways. Scholars list *adequacy, equity, and efficiency* as the characteristics of a good revenue system (Knoeppel et al., 2013).

It is clear, however, that there is little agreement between the two major perspectives about US education when it comes to the "better" established by education and when it comes to funding for the education that ensures "better."

The mechanisms and ideological foundations of privatization education envision "better" as a cost and as an outcome limited to those worthy enough to engage in its pursuit. The "better" envisioned by traditional education and the funding required to realize "better" emerge from sufficient funding that engages all students with dynamic instruction that fosters *how to think*, social justice, and pursuit of the common good in democracy (Swensson et al., 2019a).

Foundation formulas crafted in each state reflect how one or the other perspective about education is enacted. Establishing a school funding system for "better" is a series of confrontations. These confrontations are between either-or iterations: efficiency or sufficiency, survival of the fittest or the common good, and less or more. Confrontations like these reflect "the competing policy goals of taxpayer equity and the provision of educational services" that tend to throw efforts to foster equity, fairness, and sufficiency out of balance (Knoeppel et al., 2013, "Using Educational Research," para. 2).

The stage is set for a discussion about the dilemmas and unfulfilled promises inherent in funding for education in the United States. In part, these result from the fact that

> the quality and quantity of educational services are determined in large measure
> by the wishes of government officials; by the pleasant or unpleasant experiences

voters have had with education in their own lives; by groups with interest in education such as parents, teachers, and administrators; and by taxpayers who seek to lower their share of the tax burden. The degree of satisfaction of students is often secondary to the concerns of taxpayers; who largely determine the extent of such services available. (Brimley et al., 2012, p. 11).

Unfulfilled promises of traditional public education and its funding deserve exploration because they represent unmet responsibilities. Any such exploration and any such examination of responsibilities unmet begin from the fact that "states are a focal point for policy discussions around school funding, as they set policies that direct billions of dollars in state funding and potentially affect decisions by school districts about how to raise and use local revenue" (Chingos and Blagg, 2017, p. v).

Divergent perspectives about "better" infest policy, decision-making, and ideology that jump-start funding for public education. Public education's future contributions to the lives of all students and to the existence of the common good will be determined by which "better" expresses how US society sees itself and how "better" is funded by public revenue.

Chapter Three

A Case Study

Weeds in Indiana's School Funding Field

To the surprise of many, one out of every five workers in Indiana is employed in manufacturing (Girardi-Schachter, 2019). To the surprise of no one, agriculture is the prevailing first impression about productivity in the state.

Hard-working farmers and bounteous yields of soybeans and corn are enduring images (along with basketball hoops affixed to barns) of the land also known as the Hoosier State. Using data, applying best practices, and focusing on service to consumers, agriculture in Indiana has a proud and enviable record of quality and success. The science of agriculture allows Indiana farmers to grow row after row of weed-free crops.

Indiana's legislators, whose constitutional responsibility is tending the field of public education, appear to ignore the lessons learned and successes earned by farmers. Where farmers are driven by data, best practices, and needs of the consumer, the state's legislators seem smitten with ideology, assumption, and disdain when working the field of traditional public education.

The legislature sows invasive funding initiatives that interfere with and reduce the financial resources available for public schools. Often heard grumbling about funding for K–12 education (constituting 54 percent of state expenditures in 2011 [Nelson and Balu, 2014]), legislators have long chafed at this burden.

This chapter examines Indiana as a case study that represents the difficulties, dilemmas, and distractions that put US traditional public schools and the students who attend them in untenable positions. Segments of this case study conveyed *in italics* convey the professional experiences and impressions of the authors, all of whom have served as leaders in Indiana school districts or as leaders in statewide educators' organizations. This leadership included sharing data, conversations, and perspectives about adequate school funding with numerous state leaders.

As this chapter will reveal, traditional public education and the funding that supports it grow in a field cluttered with weeds. Instead of harvesting a bumper crop of high-performing public schools, the funding programs spread by the Hoosier legislature yield a field clogged with the weeds of inequity and inadequacy

PREPARING THE FIELD: FUNDING FOR EDUCATION IN INDIANA

Indiana's economy is dependent on the degree to which the legislature funds public education in accordance with the state's constitution. Hoosier economists confirm the value of public education to a state's economy (Hicks, 2019).

Indiana's constitution clearly delineates the legislature's duty to "provide by law, for a general and uniform system of Common Schools, wherein tuition shall be without charge, and equally open to all" (Indiana Constitution, 1851, Article 8). The legislature undertakes this duty when, every two years, the state's budget is promulgated.

Two items account for a disproportionate amount of the revenue allocated through the state budget: Medicare payments to the federal government and funding for public education. Always problematic in one way or another, school finance bedevils state legislators for its total impact on state budgets and for its presence as a target of both school supporters and tax protesters.

Proponents of less government and lower taxes—at one point in history aligned with the "Tea Party"—bombarded less experienced, younger, members of Indiana's legislature with prepackaged legislation created by the Council of State Legislators. Among the effects of this barrage was interest in and legislation for so-called Kindergarten Scholarships. This initiative was the harbinger of Indiana's crop of weeds in the field of public education.

Indiana's foundation formula provides a minimum per-pupil amount for public education and represents the legislature's effort to fulfill its constitutional duty in the twenty-first century. During fiscal year 2016, for example, this amount was $5,088 (Moon and Stewart, 2016). "Additional funding is calculated through a complexity formula that takes into account the socioeconomic level of each district's students" (Moon and Stewart, 2016, p, 3).

National Trends Raining on Indiana's Field

National trends affect Hoosier funding for public education. One such trend is free market theory (Friedman, 1955). The influence of free market theory on members of Indiana's General Assembly inspired the growth of school funding mechanisms like charter schools and vouchers.

Free market theory for education blossomed in the dubious but ballyhooed assertions found in A Nation at Risk (National Commission on Excellence in Education, 1983). Claiming that public education in the United States was a failed institution, the tangled vines of exaggerations and innuendo within this publication eschewed data and fended off credible scrutiny. Savransky (2017) chronicles the enduring impact of free market theory by sharing the thinking of the US Secretary of Education who portrayed traditional public schools as Stone Age relics and supporters of this perspective as the equivalent of flat-earthers.

Between allegations that US public educators are inept and offering choice education as a cure for the malaise endemic to traditional public schools, free market theory (e.g., choice, competition, efficiency, less government) became the brand name of schooling preferred by policymakers eager to shift or remove the fiscal burden established by constitutional imperatives for public education.

This theory, like an invasive plant, blossomed in the form of privatization education (e.g., charter schools, vouchers, virtual education, tax credits). Beginning with the first charter schools in Wisconsin during the early 1990s, legislators put free market theory into practice so that resources formerly devoted to traditional public schools were repurposed to deliver choice education.

Elsewhere in the National Field

Under the auspices of the George H. W. Bush administration in the late 1980s, education summits brought together governors and CEOs to develop standards that articulated what students ought to know and be able to do as a result of teaching and learning at every grade level. These standards were shared with all states. "Goals 2000" emerged from this collaboration as a set of standards that all public schools were to reach by the year 2000.

Following suit, the Bill Clinton administration promulgated a standards-based vision for education reflected in the 1994 reauthorization of the ESEA that required all states to establish rigorous standards for teaching and learning in all subjects and at all grade levels.

Nationally during the 1980s and 1990s, public educators worked to define what was known as outcomes-based education or OBE (Spady, 1994). OBE was a widely marketed attempt to improve student achievement via teaching standards designed by educators.

At the turn of the twenty-first century, the National Council of Teachers of Mathematics published standards for teaching and learning. At the same time, "Goals 2000" education summits, launched during the Clinton administration,

galvanized standards-based learning and assessment to No Child Left Behind
(NCLB) legislation in 2001 during the George W. Bush administration.

NCLB not only established annual standardized testing, and the results of
these tests, as the primary determinants of student achievement and school
district success, but this legislation also mandated that 100 percent of all students demonstrate achievement success—generally referred to as "adequate
yearly progress" (AYP)—by the year 2014 (Lee, 2004).

The nation's infatuation with privatization, choice, and standards gained
momentum. Legislation and funding (both statewide and federal) supported
privatization mechanisms (e.g., charter schools, vouchers). Voucher programs as of 2018, for instance, were in place in fifteen states and used to
enroll 181,175 students in private schools (Waddington and Berends, 2018).

Back Home Again

The abundant weeds now growing throughout Indiana's public education
were sown in 1973 when a bill passed by the legislature and signed by the
governor froze property taxes. At that time, property taxes were the major
source of revenue for public education. Also in 1973, legislation passed that
required public schools to enter into collective bargaining. In one dramatic
year, legislation froze the capacity of school districts to increase revenue and
insinuated long-range cost increases into all budgets by mandating collective
bargaining.

*Almost forty years later in 2011, the legislature eliminated a pathway used
by teachers to increase earnings. No longer were either advanced degrees
earned by public educators, or prior years of experience as an educator,
permitted to increase salaries.*

*Also in 2011, the Indiana Supreme Court ruled that "tax credits" were
a legal source of revenue for vouchers. Within days of this pronouncement,
the General Assembly, State School Chief, and Governor engineered a vast
expansion of Indiana's crop of voucher programs and charter schools.*

SCHOOL FUNDING IN INDIANA: PROMISES, PROMISES

States often initiate privatization education amid a flurry of promises. Indiana's state leaders announced, for instance, that there would be caps on the
number of vouchers when the state's program was first introduced.

Hoosier legislators also proclaimed that traditional public schools would
receive a fiscal windfall because the cap on the number of vouchers ensured
that the state dollars allocated to fund vouchers would not be spent completely. The difference between the total funding allocated for vouchers and

the actual expenditures arising from capped voucher enrollments was touted as additional funding for traditional public education.

Indiana's Governor, Mitch Daniels, in his first State of the State address shared several promises about education. The governor let it be known in a State of the State speech that Indiana would be establishing "kindergarten as early as they do in other states, moving more of school corporations' spending to instruction, and increasing Charter Schools."

As if anticipating how these promises would play out for teaching and learning in Indiana, a veteran legislator spoke about the impact of a newly elected group of Hoosier legislators aligned with the so-called Tea Party. "It will be a sad day when this group takes control of fiscal spending policy in the state, especially for the future of public schools."

On the Alert for Free Market Weeds

School leaders from Wisconsin issued a stark warning when they called one of the authors. The warning called attention to the host of free market weeds that could erupt in the field of public education following a promise to increase charter schools. School leaders from the Badger State bemoaned an infestation of privatization and legislation for vouchers. With the support of Wisconsin's governor and the endorsement of the state's legislature, reductions in the state's already underfunded foundation formula for public schools were underway.

Teacher walkouts in Wisconsin and demonstrations at the state capitol told the tale of an unforgiving climate for traditional public education. The phone call concluded with an ominous predication: The same ideological and funding infestation was headed for the Hoosier State.

With Thanks to General Patton

As General George Patton is said to have crowed after victory in a battle against Nazi General Erwin Rommel in North Africa during World War II, "I read your book!" A historic example of the epigram, "forewarned is forearmed," Patton's study of Rommel's book on military tactics paid off. In the same way, knowing what was coming to upend funding for public education gave Indiana's school leaders information to defend against an impending invasion.

Initially, Indiana's public educators, with the help of stalwart defenders of traditional public education in the Indiana legislature, fended off the attempt to create vouchers and charter schools. The first legislation introduced to fulfill the promises made during the governor's speech, the "Kindergarten

Scholarship" bill, was cloaked in benign images of cute little kids with mortar boards teetering on their heads and slipping down over their eyes.

Seen as a Trojan Horse for choice education and allocation of revenue to fuel a free market invasion, this bill was thwarted for two years by data and details organized by a coalition of Indiana educational organizations (e.g., teachers' associations, university teacher preparation programs, associations of school counselors, principals, and superintendents).

Unperturbed by the delay, Indiana's governor removed the cap on the number of charter schools in 2009. Governor Daniels' comment at the time the cap was eliminated constituted both a new promise and a threat: "If this is the end of public education as we know it, I say thank goodness" (Ellis, 2010, p. 217).

As the promise of a cap on the number of charter schools fell by the wayside, other promises also disappeared. Hopes for state funding for full-day kindergarten in public schools evaporated. Indiana's General Assembly failed to fund full-day kindergarten. The estimated cost of $140 million to finance this aspect of traditional public education could not withstand the claims of less cost bandied about by adherents of free market schooling.

Winning the Battle But Losing the War

Eventually, free market theory proponents won the day in the Indiana General Assembly. Public educators in the Hoosier State were confronted by declining support from the General Assembly at the same time that federal legislation and mandates (e.g., NCLB, AYP) imposed an escalation of test score–based targets on public schools. No commensurate increase in funding was provided for the academic support required to help all students reach these academic performance numbers.

At the same time, the Indiana Department of Education undermined progress toward AYP by frequently rewriting state standards. Sudden, fundamental, and complicated alterations of testing standards were implemented each time Indiana public schools got closer to realizing the academic proficiencies required by an existing set of state standards.

These conglomerations of revised state standards were nothing less than a series of unfunded mandates. Funding shortfalls failed to allow for staff development or for additional instructional support for students. The Indiana Association of Public School Superintendents joined educators across the state in expressing frustration with the consequences of the actions taken by the legislature to undercut traditional public education.

INDIANA'S FIRST PRIVATIZATION CROP

The onslaught of free market theory and funding for choice or privatization schooling overwhelmed the defenses of Indiana's public education when one-party rule (one party gained control of both houses of the legislature in 2009) became a reality. From this one-way-on-the-highway legislative state of affairs came legislation that struck at the heart of traditional public schools.

Using an unbreakable free market pipeline to supply model bills that served as fill-in-the-blank legislation, Indiana's legislature passed a "tuition tax credit" to provide funding support for nonpublic schools. Contributions from individuals and corporations were a form of tax abatement allowed by this legislation.

Tuition tax credits funded choice education when the state sent checks to families with children attending private schools. Mimicking tax credits, Indiana also enacted the "Indiana Choice Scholarship Program" that legislators proclaimed would get "poor kids out of failing schools."

In bringing forward the Indiana Choice Scholarship Program, state leaders established characteristics for a student's participation in the program that seemed to promise students in poverty genuine options for otherwise unobtainable private schooling. Family income level and prior enrollment in traditional public school were introduced as necessary qualifications for a voucher under this program (Waddington and Berends, 2018).

The Indiana Choice Scholarship Program

The Indiana Choice Scholarship (ICS) Program was established in 2011 to provide vouchers to pay private school tuition. Emerging from one of the model bills manufactured by the American Legislative Exchange Council (ALEC), the ICS Program grew and became the largest voucher program in the United States (Waddington and Berends, 2018).

The promises made when this program was introduced evaporated in the same way that promises about the Kindergarten Scholarship program disappeared. "Each year since the program's inception, eligibility criteria and the number of available vouchers have expanded" (Moon and Stewart, 2016, p. 1). As of the 2017–2018 school year, 35,458 students in 318 private schools in Indiana received a voucher under this program.

LEGISLATIVELY MODIFIED EDUCATION

Indiana's state leaders denied that funding for privatization education had a negative impact on revenue for traditional public education. Ironically, this denial amounted to turning a deaf ear to reports generated at the behest of the General Assembly itself. These reports showed the negative impact of voucher funding on overall revenue for traditional public education in Indiana (Ellis, 2010).

Other voices, it turns out, had the attention of the General Assembly. Listening to educational pundits from business, industry, and third-party entities such as ALEC, Indiana's elected officials found new ways to modify funding for public education.

Governors of several Midwestern states (including Indiana's Mitch Daniels) promoted what was referred to as the 65% Solution. Endorsed by a nationally known business executive, the 65% Solution asserted that traditional public schools should be mandated to spend 65 percent of all funding on instruction.

Indiana's leaders claimed that public schools spent only 61 percent of state revenue on classrooms and, therefore, wasted state funding. State leaders claimed that each 1 percent of school funding put back into the classroom by school districts to reach the 65 percent goal would yield 100 million new dollars with which to pay teachers and reduce class sizes.

The 65 Percent Straw Man

The claim that public schools failed to use tax dollars at a rate (e.g., 65 percent) that was touted as sufficient, efficient, and effective for student learning was a straw man. A goal without evidence to support its value, this alleged solution was promoted with such intensity by state leaders that traditional public school educators spent inordinate amounts of time refuting its accuracy. Public conversation about education in Indiana descended into an exchange of accusations and refutations about the instructional accuracy of a mythic, data-free, bottom line.

The accusation that Indiana school districts failed to deliver the excellence implied by the 65% Solution led to an analysis by Financial Management, Analysis, and Reporting Plan (FINMars). FINMars was a group mandated by the General Assembly and chaired by the Indiana Department of Education (IDOE) and one of the authors participated in the group's four-month analysis.

To determine the extent to which Indiana's public schools did or did not align with the 65% Solution, FINMars analyzed the Object Codes in the bud-

gets of every public school district in the state. Object Codes, standardized and required by the state in all school district budgets, designate how state funding is spent for specified purposes.

The findings from this analysis of Object Code published in a FINMars report showed that 85 percent of the General and Pre-School Education Fund was already being spent on instruction and instructional support across all public school districts. To adjust this spending down to 65 percent would require altering, reducing, or eliminating budgeted revenue for

> *Debt Service, Capital Projects, most Transportation and replacement and operation funds, Retirement Severance Bond Funds, most of school lunch costs, and some expenditures from the Textbook Rental Fund (money which cannot legally be used for instruction)"* (Ellis, 2010, p. 208).

A classic example of a red herring, the 65% Solution constitutes an example of the misdirection inherent in adult-centric intentions for public education.

Public Funding for Less Achievement

Contending over the 65% Solution gave Indiana's leaders cover and support for choice schooling mushroomed. The growth of public funding for privatization education facilitated two outcomes. First, the impact of receiving a voucher on student achievement is clear. Scholars "found no consistent evidence that vouchers promote increased academic achievement among low-income recipients" (Waddington and Berends, 2018, p. 784). Alongside the failure of millions of state dollars devoted to privatization education to improve or increase the achievement of enrolled Hoosier students, between 2010 and 2020 "inflation-adjusted spending on both higher education and K–12 has dropped" (Hicks, 2020).

Insufficient funding for and ideological intensity about public education in the Hoosier State affect instructional initiatives. For example, a few Indiana legislators persistently proposed that *cultural competency* become a curricular and instructional requirement throughout Indiana's public schools. On the "Why Cultural Competence?" page of its website, the National Education Association (NEA) defines cultural competence as "the ability to understand the within-group differences that make each student unique, while celebrating the between-group variations that make our country a tapestry" (n.d.).

Indiana's Department of Education offers materials, training, and websites as resources for culturally competent classrooms. State statutes mandate incorporating cultural competency in the school plan required of each school. But no funding accompanies these resources, and revenue is not made available to accommodate the learning needs of students to engage with cultural competency materials and lessons.

The Original "Individualized" Funding for Education in Indiana

Indiana's public educators often mused about the relationship between the direction of funding for public education and individuals serving in the legislature. When Hoosier legislators began to deliberate the funding formula for each biennial budget, speculation abounded as school district leaders hypothesized about the likelihood of decreasing or increasing funding levels. During the decades of reliance on property taxes for school funding, school leaders could be heard grimly acknowledging the likelihood of static or decreasing funding when a local legislator owned substantial amounts of property.

In the face of this version of "individualization" of education funding, school leaders made a point to court local legislators whose role or seniority in the statehouse had an impact on school funding. In some cases, educators felt that their informal lobbying played to a legislator's perception of his or her individual power, and in other cases, educators knew that keeping a legislator informed gave that lawmaker data and details helpful in the struggle to sustain adequate funding for public schools.

Regardless of whether or how legislators and educators interacted about school funding, state senators and representatives held the purse strings and had the authority to divvy up funding as they saw fit.

The individualized practices of Indiana's legislators are not unique. In Pennsylvania, for example, "33 of the 37 lawmakers who represent the 21 districts that received extra funds are legislative leaders, committee chairs, vice chairs or secretarie'" (Black, 2019, p. 1411).

AT HARVEST TIME: A "REFERENDUM STATE"

Diverted and divided, funding for traditional public schools across the Hoosier State fell as privatization education siphoned away dollars. Voucher funding for students whose families were already able to pay for private education and tax credit "scholarship" dollars that never made it into the state's funding for education ($160 million in 2018–2019) reduced the funding available to public schools.

Shortly before the start of the Great Recession of 2008, Indiana's General Assembly shifted the cost of education from local to state-based resources by changing from a property tax base to a sales tax base" (Moon and Stewart,

2016, p. 3). This manipulation opened the door to a free market for education and for a roller coaster funding ride. Not only is a sales tax base less stable than a property tax base, but this change coincided with the beginning of the Great Recession and a precipitous drop in sales tax collections that led to a dramatic reduction in funding for public schools (Moon and Stewart, 2016).

Compounding this revenue reduction, Indiana's governor, Mitch Daniels, announced in December of 2009 that the state would not provide $300 million to traditional public schools starting the next month (Carden, 2009). In the middle of the school year, school districts were given thirty days to adjust their budgets.

A Fiscal About-Face

Declining state revenues for education—sales tax collections throughout Indiana were affected negatively as the Great Recession took hold of the economy—alongside the loss of funding dictated by state leadership put pressure on school districts, of course, but also on state legislators. Not only did underfunding continue to visit fiscal problems on Indiana's public schools but the recession and the state's absconding with $300 million also raised an alarm among educators and parents and caregivers that legislators heard.

Funding diverted and divided, national economic problems, and state-engineered budget reductions had a dramatic effect on the field of public education in Indiana. When the harvest of these fiscal weeds came in, Indiana became a "Referendum State."

Indiana's leaders performed the equivalent of a fiscal about-face. The legislature gave approval to school districts to hold referendums that, if approved by local voters, taxed property to add to the per-pupil funding provided by the state. This swift turnaround made Indiana into what educators referred to as a "Referendum State." The harvest signaled the return of inequities between localities because high-wealth districts were in a much better position to pass a referendum than low-wealth districts.

The "good old days" of inequitable funding of districts in Indiana and the resulting inadequacy of teaching and learning that attends unfair funding returned to the Hoosier State. The more things changed about school funding in Indiana, the more they stayed the same.

Increased Funding for Privatization Education

As local school districts mounted referendums to compensate for underfunding from the state's funding formula, state leaders imposed decisions that promised additional shortfalls for public school funding.

For example, the caps that the state formerly put on the number of vouchers were eradicated in 2013–2014. The cap on the amount of a voucher for students in grades K–8 ($4,800) was removed by the legislature in 2015–2016. The requirement that voucher-accepting students had to attend a traditional public school before enrolling in a private school disappeared.

Disappearing enrollment requirements and evaporating caps on vouchers represented significant funding increases for privatization and parallel funding losses for traditional public education. The number of vouchers rose from 7,500 (the "capped" total in 2011–2012) to a total of 32,686 after the cap was removed in 2013–2014 (Moon and Stewart, 2016).

Initial estimates showed an annual loss of $3.8 million for traditional public schools because the elimination of the cap on the voucher amount for students in grades K–8 was "sourced from the tuition support appropriation" (Legislative Services Agency, 2015b, as cited in Moon and Stewart, 2016, p. 6).

Researchers found that Indiana's vouchers became a resource for parents and caregivers whose children had always attended private schools (Moon and Stewart, 2016). Studies also revealed that the preponderance of schools receiving voucher funds were religiously affiliated (Weaver, 2018).

Knowing which way the fiscal wind blows for education funding in Indiana is indicated by scholars of economics who noted in 2020 that "the drop-off in college attendance in Indiana seems to accompany broad efforts to downplay the importance of both K–12 and college education" (Hicks, 2020).

FUNDING REFLECTIONS: INDIANA'S SCHOOL PICTURE

Funding for Indiana's general and uniform system of education yields schooling and educational outcomes that include:

- Indiana students who attend a school with a high-minority enrollment are more than twice as likely as students in low-minority schools to be taught by inexperienced teachers (Kids Count 2020, p. 71).
- "Indiana, overall, has the third highest reported rate of educators leaving the profession not related to retirement" (Kids Count 2020, p. 71).
- More than 1.1 million students enrolled in grades K–12 in Indiana during 2019; 88 percent of these students attended traditional public schools, while 4.5 percent enrolled in public charter schools, 4.4 percent attended nonpublic schools, and 3.2 percent were enrolled in School Choice Voucher schools (Kids Count 2020, p. 77).

- Indiana's high school graduation rate fell almost three percentage points between 2014 and 2019 (Kids Count 2020, p. 89).
- Indiana's charter public schools are almost three times more likely to earn an "F" grade from the state's accountability system and almost five times more likely to earn an "F" grade from the national accountability system (Kids Count 2020, p. 92).
- Amid the coronavirus pandemic of 2020, Indiana received more than $61 million in discretionary funding from the federal government for its schools. The governor's announced plan for this revenue prioritizes improved distance or online learning capabilities among educators but includes "no clear strategy for increasing the number of broadband subscriptions in wired communities where fees can be unaffordable for low-income families" (Fittes, 2020).

As a representative of funding for education across the United States, this case study suggests the dilemmas and disconnections that afflict teaching and learning. Funding, as this one state reveals, is the essential fuel, and the primary bone of contention, for both major perspectives about education in the nation. A broader view of this reality in the next chapter opens the door to fundamental difficulties faced by students and society from the nation's inadequate and inequitable funding formulas.

Chapter Four

What Does School Funding Pay for?

At first glance, funding for US education pays for the obvious: teaching and learning. Basic instructional "purchases" (e.g., salary and benefits for teachers and staff; staff development) establish US education as "the bedrock of an informed democracy and the bridge to lifelong learning" (Villanueva, 2019, "Charter School Funding," para. 1). The vastly different intentions of traditional public education or those of privatization education ensure that school funding pays for fundamentally different teaching and learning.

Purchases on behalf of one major perspective or the other yield different goods (e.g., the common good, an individual good). The purchasing power required to buy these goods is provided when a foundation formula sets "a base funding level that is deemed necessary for a basic or adequate education, determines the required amount of local effort that has to be put towards raising the funds, and uses state funds to cover the shortfall" (Verstegen 2011, 2016; Verstegen and Jordan 2009, as cited in Weathers and Sosina, 2019, p. 9).

A foundation formula not only constitutes purchasing power but also portends "an equitable fiscal partnership between the state as a whole and the individual school system charged with the responsibility and privilege of operating the public schools" (Mort and Ruesser, 1951, p. 382). Because what is paid for by a foundation formula yields fundamentally different *goods* associated with each major perspective, the likelihood that this partnership leads to either similar schooling or equitable funding is limited.

The purpose of this chapter is to explore the expectations and assumptions that accompany the purchasing power facilitated by foundation formulas. Purchases made in the name of funding for US education help define the qualities and the quandaries embedded in schooling in the United States. Decisions made by taxpayers, lawmakers, citizens, parents, caregivers, and policymakers determine what is purchased for US education.

The discussion in this chapter will examine legislative super shoppers, educational gerrymandering, the great school funding game, cooking-up funding formulas, and purchasing power. All these topics shed light on what's paid for when funding purchases either privatization education or traditional public education.

SUPER SHOPPERS: STATE LEGISLATURES

Paying for education is a process (setting a budget, creating a list, using the list to buy quality items, and putting purchases to good use) that encapsulates a legislature's activation of policy in a funding formula that permits allocation of revenue for education. Since the middle of the twentieth century, many states assumed responsibility for more than half of the revenue raised and allocated for traditional public education (Corcoran et al., 2017). As a result, legislatures exercise a unique authority and capacity when it comes to this process: the power to gerrymander.

Educational Gerrymandering

Legislatures are super shoppers for education. Endowed with constitutional authority for education and its funding, the fifty state legislatures have experience with dividing, prioritizing, allocating, and implementing plans and programs. This power to arrange, divide, and organize to express a legislature's authority has been referred to as *gerrymandering*. Gerrymandering usually refers to the manipulation of the boundaries for voting districts that results in a configuration of voters likely to cast ballots for the political party that manipulated the district boundaries.

Black (2019) applies this tendency of legislatures to manipulate and identifies *educational gerrymandering* as a close cousin of the political phenomenon:

> Educational gerrymandering includes: arbitrarily driving down the estimated cost of educating students; consistently picking low supplements for at-risk students; conveniently excluding inflation increases and other fixed costs over time; and shifting excessive and unrealistic funding burdens onto local districts (Black, 2019, p. 1396).

Legislators wield immense power when gerrymandering funding for education. Divvying up a foundation formula—in response to the wealth or racial makeup of a school district—is a frequent legislative endeavor. Stacking the deck to manipulate funding—educational gerrymandering—is a game of chance in which the legislature, like the "house" in any casino, holds the winning hand.

THE GREAT SCHOOL FUNDING GAME

Funding either traditional public education or privatization education is a high-stakes game for state legislatures. Although this great school funding game is played differently in each state, there are constants that affect play.

The first constant, as Baker et al. (2016) note, is that education is labor-intensive. The hundreds of billions of dollars spent annually across the nation determine the number of personnel, the wages for personnel, and the quality of personnel in public schools. Personnel "purchases" enact the intentions, goals, and outcomes sought on a day-to-day basis by either of the two major perspectives of US education.

The second constant that influences the school funding game is the push for what scholars refer to as *resource-free reforms*, which are invoked so that "the connection between revenue, spending, and real, tangible resources are often ignored or, worse, argued to be irrelevant" (Baker et al., 2016, p. 3). Legislatures and free market schooling advocates often collaborate to undercut investment in public education or to add mandates for public schools without adding revenue.

The third constant in play as legislatures shuffle the deck before dealing out school funding is provided by what amounts to a pit boss. In this case, unlike at a casino where the pit boss is present to oversee the game's reliability, the pit boss overseeing school funding for choice education is an outside entity like a foundation, a management organization, or an ideologically oriented organization like ALEC. This pit boss ensures the game's vulnerability.

A Pit Boss for the Game

ALEC is "best described as a 'corporate bill mill' that helps conservative state legislators become a vessel for advancing special interest legislation" (Fischer, 2013, p. 26). The ideological substitution preferences about education alive and well in state legislatures are tapped by the model bills ground out by this mill. Privatization education and its funding are established by legislation fashioned after the templates provided by ALEC.

Legislators from all fifty states are members of ALEC serving alongside various corporate executives and policymakers (Swensson et al., 2019a). The titles of model bills drafted by ALEC members advertise the agenda of this pit boss for the great school funding game (e.g., *Parental Choice Scholarship*

Act, Virtual Schools Act, Great Schools Tax Credit Act). Scholars ascribe the motivation behind these bills as a belief that "'public education is one of the last vestiges of socialism in America'" (Fischer, 2013, p. 28). Choice school mechanisms put into play by these and other bills introduce privatization education as the antithesis of traditional public schooling.

Dealing from the Middle of the Deck

If there is a middle of the deck for the school funding game, it is at the point where a state constitution is used by legislators to manipulate the boundaries of taxation for education. Dealing from the middle of the deck to control funding for education and what it can purchase has a long history.

Missouri, for example, amended its constitution in 1865 to include an article that mandated the state to provide free schools in all townships. A scant ten years later, yet another amended constitution "deleted the language mandating equality of education as a right for all Missouri children" (Rowe, 2010, p. 1044).

More than a century and a half later, Missouri's constitution delimits funding for education as a cost instead of an investment. Contemporary wording sets forth that "in no case shall there be set apart less than twenty-five percent of the state revenue, exclusive of interest and sinking fund, to be applied annually to the support of the free public schools" (Rowe, 2010, p. 1045). Legal scholars interpret this constitutional stipulation of *at least 25 percent of state revenue* as a high-water mark that no future legislature need surpass to meet the responsibility for funding public education (Rowe, 2010).

Constitutional boundary changes like those in Missouri illustrate how the great school funding game deals from the middle of the deck. Wording in a state constitution can be amended and amended again; cards are pulled from out of nowhere to alter what is or is not paid for. The constitutional cards in play during the twenty-first century in Missouri reveal how state revenue for education can be restricted.

A PINCH OF THIS, A DOLLOP OF THAT: COOKING SCHOOL FUNDING

Educational gerrymandering means that legislatures are in position to incorporate, or withhold, ingredients while funding formulas are cooked up. Intentions, economic conditions, taxpayer concerns, political priorities, and ideological imperatives all are among the ingredients that legislators choose to create a recipe that pays for school funding. Legislators are responsible, also, for the "portion size" served to each school district once the funding formula comes out of the legislative oven.

The dish that emerges, the funding formula, reflects the ingredients chosen and the use of several different legislative cooking techniques:

- *Just a dash of adequacy:* Legislative chefs can pretend to add just a dash of adequacy while creating an artificially low estimate for a state's base student cost in a funding formula. Chefs in the Kansas legislature modeled this culinary art by identifying, then allocating, the revenue adequate for the state's "successful schools." But the successful schools identified by the legislature were nothing more than a select subset of the state's schools that "were 'merely the best, or the most efficient, of the constitutionally inadequate' schools" (Black, 2019, p.1397).
- *Sorry, we're fresh out:* Legislators in the funding kitchen can pretend that there are no more ingredients available for the funding recipe. One example of this technique is offered in New York where, despite a court ruling that funding for low-income students required a 50 percent weight, "the state later chose to apply a thirty-five percent weight instead" (Black, 2019, p. 1404). By pretending the cupboard was bare New York funding chefs reduced the state's funding obligation by $1 billion.
- *Order takeout:* Although most legislatures have increased the state's portion of revenue in the funding formula, there are states (e.g., Illinois, Missouri) where the "funding formula placed a [significant] burden on local school districts by increasing their responsibility [to fund] public schools" (Rowe, 2010, p. 1039). Instead of taking on the funding burden for public education at the state level, this cooking technique is the equivalent of a restaurant ordering takeout from the dining room down the street then serving it as their own cuisine.
- *Uninvolved cooks spoil the broth:* Legislatures take advantage of the fact that both state and local decision-makers can be involved in cooking up funding. State legislators, as a result, can orchestrate the extent to which local "chefs" must contribute to school funding.

    This example of what one scholar references as the *bifurcation* of funding resources means that "the state will not spread the full cost of public education for all districts across all districts. It will only spread a portion of that cost" (Black, 2019, p. 1407).

    The result is that high-wealth districts can generate the funding necessary for adequacy, but low-wealth districts are left to deal with underfunding created by multiple uninvolved cooks with access to insufficient ingredients for a successful funding dish.

- *The perfect recipe?* "Massachusetts is the only state to reimburse districts when students leave for charter schools" (Stillings-Candal and Ardon, 2019, "How School Funding Works," para. 7). Adjusting to a loss of enrollment and the resulting statistical increase in costs of instruction, Massachusetts applies "a reimbursement formula in which districts receive money to offset the tuition payments they make to charter schools" (Stillings-Candal and Ardon, 2019, "How School Funding Works," para. 6).

    For six years on a descending scale, traditional public schools receive a percentage of the tuition they pay out to each charter where a former student enrolled. The "catch" in what appears to be a recipe for funding both perspectives about US education is that the payment to districts for students lost to charter schools depends on full state funding of charter reimbursements. The chefs ensure that this line item in the Massachusetts budget is perpetually underfunded.

- *Sounds like "stone soup" to me.* Indiana's approach to easing the costs for traditional public education after students enroll in privatization education—unlike that of Massachusetts—is a modern adaptation of the folk tale known as *Stone Soup*.

    This tale recounts how a newly arrived stranger in a village sets up a large kettle of boiling water. The stranger announces he's making stone soup, which, although unbelievably delicious on its own, could be improved if someone in the village contributed just a couple of potatoes. The result of this entreaty, and others that lead to more contributions, is a marvelous concoction sufficient to feed the entire village.

    Indiana's "take" on this tale is to contribute nothing when students leave traditional public school. Hoosier policymakers assume that even though annual revenue is not known until the summer before an academic year, public school districts will immediately cut costs to make ends meet. The funding "soup" served, in this case, is the revenue equivalent of boiled rocks.

PURCHASING POWER:
PAYING FOR TRADITIONAL PUBLIC EDUCATION

Paying for quality instruction in traditional public education entails purchases that include "professional development, instructional coaches, and teacher planning time" (Larkin, 2016, p. 20; Partelow et al., 2018). Fiscal support for traditional public education not only puts teacher assistants in place to aid students with special needs but also provides for instruction using relevant materials and equipment in lab classes for science, instrumental music, art, and physical education (Lafer, 2018).

Sufficient funding for public education focused on instruction yields important learning benefits for students. "The states ranked highest on *Education Week's* 2017 Quality Counts K–12 achievement index have per-pupil spending well above the national average of $11,454" (Partelow et al., 2018, "Money Matters in Education," para. 5).

Public funding for traditional public education entails several purchases that can facilitate and enhance instruction and learning. Among these are public accountability, legal safeguards for students and parents, or fiscal monitoring by outside entities.

School finance reforms (SFRs) ordered by state courts, reframe foundation formulas and permit public schools to purchase instructional program improvements including smaller class sizes, after-school tutoring, or extension of the school day or school year (Jackson et al., 2016; Weathers and Sosina, 2019).

Purchasing power for traditional public education means paying for educators and school support staff. Nearly 80 percent of public school expenditures on a per-pupil basis in 2015 were accounted for by staff salaries and benefits (Partelow et al., 2018, "Lack of Funding," para. 1). Revenue, the "funds received and potentially able to be spent" (Baker et al., 2012, p. 6) determines what a school district can pay to establish class sizes, wages, staffing ratios, and other elements of instruction (Baker, Farrie, and Sciarra, 2016).

School Funding as an Investment

For decades, studies have shared the critical importance of sufficient funding as an investment to ensure adequate instruction that meets the needs of all students. Research indicates that better funding for school districts attracts "teachers with higher levels of education, more experience, and higher scores on competency tests; these teachers, in turn, seem to generate better achievement scores among students" (Darling-Hammond and Post, 2000; Elliott, 1998; Ferguson, 1991; Ferguson and Ladd, 1996, as cited in Biddle and Berliner, 2002, p. 58).

Partelow et al. (2018) report details of a study in 2018 that found "that the NAEP test score gap decreased in states that passed school finance reforms to make funding more equitable but remained the same in states that did not" ("Money Matters," para. 3).

Despite this and other evidence that supports the value of adequate funding for traditional public schools in a state, foundation formulas frequently fail to deliver revenue that corresponds to these findings. Researchers have discovered that "only nine states provide the highest poverty districts the funds they need to achieve average outcomes" (Black, 2019, p. 1420). New York's state budget for 2019–2020, for example, allocated more than $250 million to private schools despite "underfunding the State's public schools by over $3 billion" (Public Funds Public Schools [PFPS], 2020a).

PURCHASING POWER: PAYING FOR CHOICE EDUCATION

Paying for choice or privatization education is an exercise in cost abatement. Free market theory holds that education is (i) a cost, not an investment and (ii) an individual good, not a public or common good. Efficient provision of this private good is facilitated when mechanisms (e.g., charter schools, vouchers, virtual schools) are both education and the purchasing power for this education (Swensson et al., 2019b). Choice education mechanisms are heralded for low cost and the delivery of hallmarks of free market theory: lower taxation, less government, and competition between schools in a marketplace.

The shopping list created by adherents of privatization education includes several items that align with the intentions of free market theory:

- "Profit-oriented charter schools allocate a smaller portion of the expenses to instructional staff" (Weber and Baker, in press, as cited in Lee, 2018, p. 13).
- "The economic rewards for high achievement as measured by standard tests are greater in the United States than in virtually all developed countries" (Hanushek, 2020, p. 5).
- Voucher programs in both Indiana and Milwaukee provide state funding largely devoted to student attendance at religious schools (Ford, 2016).
- Nationally, less than 50 percent of voucher programs include legal protections against racial discrimination and "even fewer states provide protections for students based on religion, sex, disability status, sexual orientation, and gender identity" (Fiddiman and Yin, 2019, "The State of US Voucher Programs," para. 2).
- "Small increases in the pupil-teacher ratio or the pupil-staff ratio can release substantial funds that might go to the compensation enhancements" (Hanushek, 2020, p. 3).
- Philadelphia's charter schools "serve fewer impoverished students, fewer English language learners, fewer students with severe disabilities, and fewer boys" (Gallo, 2014, p. 227) compared to traditional public schools in the city.
- In Texas, funding formulas "end up funding every charter as though it were in a small district with an average daily attendance of 824 students"

(Villanueva, 2019, p. 1). This funding bonanza for charters means that 95 percent of the traditional public school students in Texas attend schools where the adjusted allotment is below that for charter schools.

- K–12 Inc., the largest national for-profit EMO providing virtual schools, tallied net profits in 2018 of "$46.4 million and total revenues of $917.7 million" (Molnar et al., 2019, "Eliminating Profiteering," para. 1).
- In 2019, Florida's governor signed a law that shifted almost $130 million away from public education to private schools; Indiana's governor signed into law a 15 percent increase in funding for the state's existing tax credit voucher program; and Mississippi's lieutenant governor attached $2 million in new voucher funding to a bill that funded construction projects undertaken by the state (PFPS, 2019a).

School Funding as a Cost

Paying for choice education is accomplished when per-pupil funding "follows" a student who enrolls in a charter school, virtual school, or private school. Voucher funding "shadows" students to private schools via pathways crafted by state policy. Through the various mechanisms of choice education, states allocate impressive sums:

- Indiana's voucher program in 2015 disbursed almost $113 million, whereas by 2017 the estimated disbursement rose to almost $174 million (Moon and Stewart, 2016).
- Between 1991 and 2013, the voucher program provided $1.6 billion in public funding (adjusted for inflation) to Milwaukee private schools (Ford, 2016).
- Between 2004 and 2014 charter schools in Pennsylvania have received $4 billion in public funds (Gallo, 2014).
- 73 percent of all students supported by vouchers in private schools are funded by programs in Florida, Indiana, Ohio, and Wisconsin which are the four largest voucher programs in the nation (US Government Accountability Office [GAO], 2016).

The purchase of lower cost in choice education is accomplished by hiring noncertified teachers, by relying on computer-based instruction, or by limiting enrollment totals and the cohorts of students permitted to enroll. Less reliance on public funds also occurs when choice schools receive private donations and contributions.

SCHOOL FUNDING: COST OR INVESTMENT?

The frenzy for low-cost education exhibited by proponents of free market theory aligns with the perception that spending for traditional public education is out of control. Alleged exorbitant costs throughout traditional public education such as "disproportionate" spending on nonteaching employees are the bane of free market thinking. An article of faith for proponents of privatization education is that "additional expenditures per pupil do not necessarily improve school performance" (Palardy, Nesbit, and Adzima, 2015, p. 293).

Scafidi (2016), evoking this mantra, contends that between fiscal years 1950 and 2009 the number of students in K–12 traditional public education rose by 96 percent but "American public schools hired personnel at a rate four times faster than the growth in student numbers over that period" (p. 122). These costs are judged to be wasteful in light of the perception that no academic improvement followed in their wake as identified by a trend assessment of National Assessment of Educational Progress (NAEP) scores (Scafidi, 2016).

Privatization Schools: Cost Reduction, Profit Expansion

Lower cost and less government are among the features of virtual schools promoted by privatization education adherents. These schools offer teaching and learning completely online. By 2017–2018, "501 full-time virtual schools enrolled 297,712 students" (Molnar et al., 2019, p. 8) throughout the US and almost 80 percent of these were virtual charter schools.

Privatization education proponents boast of less cost achieved in virtual schools that report "having 2.7 times as many students per teacher (44) compared to the national average" (Molnar et al., 2019, p. 9). Economy-of-scale maximizes reduced cost when the number of choice schools expands. Increased enrollment at choice schools, facilitated by the growth of mechanisms (e.g., vouchers, tax abatements) that fund these schools, encourages for-profit choice education.

"Within a decade of the first charter school legislation being passed, for-profit education management organizations (EMOs) became the largest players in the charter school sector" (Baker and Miron, 2015, p. 7).

Profit-making EMOs (ninety-seven distinct entities as of 2011–2012) operated hundreds of charter schools that served more than five hundred thousand students (Lee, 2018). During 2014–2015, almost one hundred for-profit EMOs operated in excess of nine hundred charter schools, while nearly three hundred not-for-profit EMOs managed more than two thousand charter schools (Baker and Miron, 2015).

When state policies ensure increasing numbers of and enrollment growth for privatization education, cost reduction is enhanced because allocations to public schools decrease (Larkin and Weiler, 2017).

School Funding Accountability

Accountability for funding public education is two-faced and double-edged. One face of accountability appears as measurement of total cost of spending and the rationing of revenue necessary for lower-cost teaching and learning. The other face of accountability appears in state audits of spending for student-centric instruction necessary to engage all students with the original power of education.

One side of the double-edged sword of accountability is standardized testing that slashes student-centric instruction in public schools. Cut away are instructional programs such as music, physical education, foreign language, and art. Left behind is the bare bones instruction known as *test prep*. This side of accountability is a blade sharpened by ideology to cut a pathway to resource-free reform and data-free assertions.

The opposite side of the sword of accountability is capable of cutting away adult-centric notions about education. Accountability from this side is to *something greater than self* that fuels student-centric instruction.

Accountable-To or Accountable-For?

Wielding the sword of accountability to defend US education as either cost or investment means battling for the supremacy of one of two determinations of accountability. These divergent determinations of the nature of accountability will be referred to as *accountable-for* and as *accountable-to.*

To be *accountable-for* is to be responsible for the success, well-being, and future of a greater good or the common good. For an individual, this determination is accountability for something beyond or greater than self. In education, this determination is a circumstance of investment. To be *accountable-to* is to be obligated to standards, preconceptions, and actions that validate only self. In education, this obligation is a circumstance of self-aggrandizement and cost abatement.

The Ironies of Cost and Investment

Cost, ironically, was levied by traditional public education as the historic failure to be *accountable-for*. For more than a century, students of color, students with special needs, and students in poverty were either excluded from traditional public schools or relegated to deliberately underfunded public schools

(Goldstein, 2015). Federal legislation and court decisions, over time, served as the levers required to confirm and implement the student-centric core of *accountable-for* in US public education.

Accountable-to, ironically, is the investment of privatization proponents in the intentions and outcomes of free market theory. Free market theory is the keystone of *accountable-to*.

Allegiance to this theory in privatization schools, as it is expressed in state statutes, precludes locally elected governance; eschews the responsive capacity for "litigation-based procedures mandated by federal law" (Naclerio, 2017, p. 1158); and avoids the enrollment requirements otherwise mandated for publicly funded education.

Accountable-to is schooling intended to benefit external entities, ideologically aligned adults, and a low-cost fiscal bottom line with only secondary regard for students. Excludable and rival, *accountable-to* schooling is the apotheosis of ironic education.

WHO WILL BUY WHAT'S FOR SALE?

What's for sale in US education is influenced by who will buy. Who will buy cost? Who will buy investment? Who will buy *accountable-to*? Who will buy *accountable-for*? What is the effect of who will buy what's for sale in teaching and learning? What students and society get when education is on sale depends on who buys what.

Who Buys What?

Who buys what is confusing, in part, because foundation formulas—the intersection between revenue from state and local sources that provides more than 90 percent of the funding for US public education—are a purchase that precedes the allocation of any funding.

Decisions are made by legislators and other policymakers to "buy" the characteristics of funding systems. These characteristics (e.g., *accountable-to*, *accountable-for*, cost, investment) predetermine what's for sale and who can buy what for public education.

After decisions are made that cost nothing, initially, the funding formulas that emerge establish price, purchasing power, and who *can buy* what for teaching and learning. Funding systems, thus, permit or restrict who can buy. The intentions of funding systems are built-in legislatively and either encourage or obstruct what school districts pay for. The extent to which education is what's paid for often depends on predeterminations such as:

- Expenditures in choice education tend to be linked to implementation of free market theory. Efficiency becomes the watchword for proponents of privatization education. Observers note that "higher public school spending figures place the spending on private school education in a more favorable light, with clear implications for the policy benefits of school vouchers" (Altemus, 2010, p. 2).
- Because at least 80 percent of the cost of education is salaries and benefits for teachers and school staff, both traditional public education and choice education tend to emphasize careful stewardship of fiscal resources. Reports generated by proponents of free market schooling have been identified as overestimating and double-counting the expenditures by traditional public education (Altemus, 2010).
- "Critics have maintained that charter schools and the [Pennsylvania] Charter School Law present a significant opportunity for profiteers to capitalize on government financing" (Gallo, 2014, p. 212).
- "Between 2000 and 2008, the Gates Foundation invested $2 billion in education reform, helping to open 2,602 small schools in 45 states, influencing over 780,000 students, in many cases closing schools and relocating students" (Barkan 2011, as cited in Rogers, 2015, p. 754).
- All revenues and expenses involved with traditional public education are subject to external audits (federal or state). In addition, federal dollars must be expended within programmatic requirements, such as student-to-teacher ratios or class size indicators, established to receive and use this revenue.

These factors influence who buys what. But, who can buy what in terms of salaries and benefits paid to traditional public educators tends to be locality specific. The purchase of instruction and instructional programs emerges from a state's funding system linked to a locality's cost of living and to the number of staff required to instruct and serve enrolled students "who live in poverty, have special needs, and are not native speakers of English" (Altemus, 2010, p. 2).

The salaries and benefits paid to privatization educators emerge from funding formulas detached from localities and linked to less-is-more, the profit motive, and other characteristics of management in choice schooling. Payment for what's sold as choice education is facilitated when funding systems provide schooling dedicated to less and to adult-centric marketplace ideology with the same revenue per-pupil provided to traditional public schools.

In the case of privatization education, foundation formula dollars that follow a student from traditional public school to a choice school are often "only a portion of the full costs of many charter schools, which often enjoy private as well as public funding" (Baker et al., 2012, p. 4).

Confusion over who buys what as a result of revenue generated by funding systems can flare up when traditional public education invests in noninstruction. For example, service on a school district's long-term debt, along with capital expenses, are among significant expenditures for a school district that do not directly pay for instruction.

Districts pay off bonds for buildings (like a mortgage for a single-family home) and spend on building maintenance, insurance, and utilities. Moreover, the roughly 10 percent of expenditures not directly related to teaching and learning are subject to market forces and other inflationary factors.

When the Federal Government Buys

Federal legislation, the ESEA, incorporated a Charter School Fund so states can fund pilot charter schools. Since the inception of the Charter School Fund in 1994, almost $4 billion has been disbursed in support of charter schools. Greene (2019a) summarized a report that discovered nearly $1 billion of this federal funding for charter schools "has been lost to fraud and waste in the charter school sector" (p. 2).

Federal regulations and rules are not enforced even if a charter receives federal funding. In Idaho, the "American Heritage Charter School emphasizes 'patriotism' with a dress code that forbids denim and head coverings" (Greene, 2019a, p. 3). In Southern California, the ACLU discovered that more than two hundred charter schools engaged in exclusionary or illegal practices.

Normally, federal funding comes with multiple requirements for accountability. However, in the case of choice education, federal accountability can be waived. For example, between 2004 and 2014 in California, more than three hundred charter schools funded directly or indirectly by federal dollars closed or never opened in the first place. Of these, "one hundred and eleven closed within a year. Seventy-five never opened at all. The cost to taxpayers—over $108 million" (Greene, 2019a, p. 3).

BUT WAIT, THERE'S MORE

Television infomercials often excite buyers with promises of two items for one low price or surprise free gifts for purchasing. Enhancement of the original purchase is about convincing buyers that *more* is essential. More aligns with the buyer's perspective. "But wait, there's more" is the catch phrase that promises what every buyer wants: more for the money.

More for proponents of privatization education enhances the original intentions associated with choice schooling: increased accountability, less cost, greater efficiency, and improved student academic performance (Baker et al., 2012). More for the advocates of traditional public education enhances the promises of quality teaching and learning, productive citizenship in US democracy, and social justice in a diverse society.

But Wait: More Is about Who

As Lafer (2018) points out, each choice education school has responsibility for only those students accepted for enrollment. In addition, when a privatization school closes, the local public school district is obligated to welcome any or all the students formerly enrolled in the failed school at any point during a school year.

It is a moral and legal obligation accepted by traditional public educators to enroll, care for, and educate every student in accordance with state regulations about the attendance boundaries, if any. Traditional public schools are responsible for all school-age children and for special needs students for several years beyond a typical graduation age.

This means that more is an efficiency achieved when any privatization school determines that "full" enrollment has been attained. Traditional public schools cannot be efficient in this way. "A district's responsibility for serving all students creates unavoidable costs" (Lafer, 2018, p. 11).

But Wait: More Is about Return on Investment

From a free market theory perspective, a return is expected when the costs of public education are paid. Return-on-investment (ROI) is the more that develops from the cost of public education if "schools deliver a return on the total revenues that they receive by using those revenues to produce learning gains that subsequently generate higher levels of lifetime earnings for students" (Wolf et al., 2014, p. 8).

The frequency with which privatization education proponents share this claim about ROI approaches a level of dissonance in light of the extensive research that indicates choice education yields academic proficiency that is, at best, less than or equal to achievement levels reached by traditional public schools (Baker et al., 2012). But wait, more from ROI is not about academic proficiency it's about fiscal advantage.

Elaborate statutory contraptions are created by states to ensure that fiscal advantage is possible even under supposedly not-for-profit choice school management. Frequently, this possibility occurs because states permit a privatization school's governing body to "establish a contract with the private management company to both directly manage the school and to engage in all subsidiary contractual agreements; in this arrangement, the employer is the management company, not the school governing board" (Baker and Miron, 2015, p. 12).

Overall, when funding for choice education siphons off funding for traditional public education, more becomes less for traditional public education. Revenue diverted away from traditional public education decreases the capacity of public schools to hire, pay, and retain quality educators.

As funding drains away, traditional public schools are forced to make drastic cuts in instructional programming with a direct effect on the quality of learning available to students. More, in this way becomes less for students and bolsters the argument that academic achievement is not a characteristic of traditional public education.

When More Yields Less

California provides an illustration of the more-means-less phenomenon. Revenue diverted to charter schools "meant that there was $1,500 less funding available per year for each child in a traditional Oakland public school" (Lafer, 2018, p. 5).

More for choice education meant that the Oakland school district in 2016–2017 faced a debt of $57 million. Less capacity for quality teaching and improvement of learning in public schools gives privatization education proponents more talking points for the alleged ineffectiveness of traditional public schools.

But Wait: More Is about Competition

Free market theory is invoked as "the best way to deliver schooling on the grounds that competition among service vendors brings about better services, lower prices and higher satisfaction" (Lee, 2018, p. 3). Vendors, under these circumstances, are private entities and management organizations (not-for-profit and for-profit) that operate charter schools, virtual schools, and private schools funded by public funds.

More is a many-faceted characteristic of competition. Competition is an intention of free market theory. More is competition between traditional public and choice education. But more also is competition that overlaps this baseline. Competition creates more that eclipses mere intentions about dollars and cents.

More and Discrimination

Competition is more in the form of discrimination that haunts state funding of education. For example, in North Carolina traditional public school enrollment is increasingly comprised of students of color, while charter school enrollment is increasingly White. More expanded ideologically between 2013 and 2015 when "North Carolina doubled its charter school funding and instituted enormous tax cuts for the wealthiest individuals in the state" (Black, 2019, p. 1418).

A study of Pennsylvania's funding formula identified racial discrimination in the state's funding distribution. Districts in the state with the heaviest concentrations of White students received "two thousand dollars more per pupil than the state's fairness formula indicates they need while predominantly minority districts receive nearly two thousand dollars less per pupil than they need" (Black, 2019, p. 1419).

More and Efficiency

Efficiency and competition are not always compatible. In Detroit, a microcosm of Michigan's status as the state with the largest number of for-profit EMOs, competition appears to trump efficiency. "The unchecked growth of charters has created a glut of schools competing for some of the nation's poorest students, enticing them to enroll with cash bonuses, laptops, raffle tickets for iPads and bicycles" (Lafer, 2018, p. 14).

Chapter Five

Are We Really Paying
for What We Get?

You get what you pay for is an adage that conveys assumptions about the relationship between the price of an item and its quality. *Caveat emptor,* or "buyer beware," is another adage that warns shoppers to pay attention to quality before they make a purchase.

Both admonitions can convey the disparate assumptions made by proponents of each of the major perspectives about US education. Adherents of each perspective—traditional public education or privatization education—believe achieving their intentions for education ensure they get what they pay for and that the opposing perspective about schooling constitutes a risky purchase.

This chapter examines if what is paid for in US education is actually what is purchased. Discussing public education as a cost or as an investment lays the groundwork for consideration of whether an impersonation of US education is actually what's being paid for. *Productivity* is explored to understand the extent to which an impersonation—a Potemkin village—is what the United States gets from school funding.

The extent to which policymakers and legislators are enticed by or engaged with this impersonation is illuminated by four significant problems endemic to funding formulas throughout the United States. The chapter concludes with a brief discussion of who's minding the store where education is purchased.

WHAT IS PAID FOR WHEN
EDUCATION IS AN INVESTMENT?

Studies undertaken between 1990 and 2008 point to the impact of school funding as payment for an investment. During this almost thirty-year time span, a host of SFRs purchased instructional and student-centric achievement programs including reductions in class size and lower teacher-to-student ratios in early childhood programs enrolling students of color and students in poverty (Baker et al., 2016).

These and other investments in teaching and learning coincided with "achievement gains for Black fourth- and eighth-grade students [that] have been substantial in mathematics in particular and that these students have outpaced their White peers" (Baker et al., 2016, p. 1). Paying for "better" creative, behavioral, and cognitive capabilities for all students is an investment in several instructional priorities:

• California's SFR referred to as local control funding formula (LCFF) "induced increases in school spending [that] led to significant increases in high school graduation rates and academic achievement, particularly among poor and minority students" (Johnson and Tanner, 2018, p. i).
• "Exogenous spending increases were associated with sizable improvements in measured school quality, including reductions in student-to-teacher ratios, increases in teacher salaries, and longer school years" (Jackson et al., 2016, p. 157).
• When SFRs are ordered by a state court, increased revenue is an investment that entails important academic improvement. "Students in low-income districts had higher mean achievement outcomes after the funding reforms, while students in high-income districts experienced no change" (Weathers and Sosina, 2019, p. 5).
• Studies of school finance reforms implemented in the 1990s in several states including Michigan, Kansas, Vermont, and Massachusetts found improved achievement in formerly low-performing districts and significant increases in test scores across different subject areas (Baker et al., 2016, p. 4).

WHAT IS PAID FOR WHEN EDUCATION IS A COST?

Cost is often a barrier to a purchase or a challenge to be reduced to allow the purchase. A "good deal" for a purchase often implies that the buyer gets something of value at an advantageous price. When funding for public education is perceived as a cost, reducing the price becomes a priority.

Free market theory invokes *accountable-to* as the role of the public sector. In the case of privatization education, reducing cost signifies a "good deal" because efficiency and competition ensue.

Privatization of education is allegiance to an ideology that prioritizes less government, less cost, and the supremacy of the individual. The role of the public sector becomes self-satisfaction engineered by those for whom *accountable-to* guarantees the equivalent of a self-fulfilling prophecy.

The good deal of charter schools, for instance, is articulated in the claim of greater productivity (compared to traditional public education) "either because they produce higher student gains at a lower cost or because they produce similar or only slightly lower student outcomes at a significantly lower cost" (Wolf et al., 2014, p. 8).

From this point of view, success is purchased when the efficiency and lower-cost associated with voucher programs in Indiana, Louisiana, and Ohio "have negative or neutral effects on student achievement" (Boser, Boser, and Roth, 2018, "An Overview," para. 2).

What is paid for on behalf of students enrolled in the voucher program in Washington, D.C., despite an annual federal investment of $60 million and voucher payments up to $8,653 or $12,981 (for elementary/middle or high school students, respectively), is a purchase with long-term effects. A 2017 report about this program found students realized no statistically significant reading improvement and lower math achievement compared to traditional public school students (Boser et al., 2018.)

Although paying for education as a cost conveys an acknowledgement that some amount of revenue always will be required from government sources, cost reduction, efficiency, and competition are promoted as productivity to ensure the lowest possible cost and the least possible purchasing power. Understanding education as a cost entails the purchase of:

- *Profit:* "As of 2014, about one in five charter students attended a school run for profit" (Barnum, 2017).
- *Built-in Disparities:* Researchers indicate the need to be concerned "that for-profit EMO-operated charter schools are more likely to serve a lower proportion of minority and disadvantaged students" (Lee, 2018, p. 3).

  In 2017–2018, the NCES illustrated the depth of this concern: 12.7 percent of students in public schools and 7.6 percent of students in private schools are in special education. The same data indicated that 10.5 percent of public school students and 2.6 percent of private school students are English-language learners (Feuerstein and Henry, 2020).
- *Marketization:* "For-profit EMO charter schools in the US were more likely to be situated in economically advantaged regions with more home-owners and fewer Title I eligible families" (Robertson, 2015, as cited in Lee, 2018, p. 6).

PAYING FOR THE IMPERSONATION OF EDUCATION

Theory and practice in business and industry have influenced US education for more than a century (Swensson and Shaffer, 2020). Striving for efficiency of leadership to emulate business productivity, educators tried to mirror the perceived success of US business and industry. Behaviors and actions of school leaders were galvanized to the pursuit of productivity. Management of orderly, quiet, rote learning was considered the height of productivity in US public education.

Productivity: The Impersonation of Teaching and Learning

Because US educators early in the twentieth century employed no original scholarship to research educational leadership, the study of management, efficiency, and productivity were borrowed from studies about leaders in business and industry. Educational leaders adapted management techniques (e.g., line and staff charts, "great man" leadership) and mimicked industrial productivity (e.g., the teacher at the front of the room, students seated at desks in rows, the Lancasterian Method).

Under the influence of free market theory in the twenty-first century, productivity continues to impersonate US education. Proponents of free market theory pose a question, and subsequently provide an answer, that supplants instruction with productivity: "What is the relative productivity of public charter schools and TPS [Traditional Public Schools], both in terms of their *cost effectiveness* and their *return on investment* (ROI)?" (Wolf et al., 2014, p. 8).

Cost effectiveness derives from a comparison between "how many test score points students gain on the 2010–11 National Assessment of Educational Progress (NAEP) for each $1000 invested in their public education" (Wolf et al., 2014, p. 8) by attending a privatized school or by attending a traditional public school. Cost effectiveness is realized if a school converts revenue, an input to education, into an outcome portrayed as an amount of learning.

Cost effectiveness is often a calculation of choice school revenue that does not incorporate funding from all sources (public and private). Cost effectiveness, thus, can be a manipulated comparison of the instructional spending of privatization education with the spending for instruction and in addition to instruction (e.g., bond payments, insurance, transportation, utilities, unfunded mandates) required in traditional public education.

ROI, the second component of productivity, is calculated via a conversion of "the learning gains developed over time by students in the public charter and TPS sectors into an estimate of the economic returns over a lifetime of students and comparing those returns to the revenue amounts invested in their education" (Wolf et al., 2014, p. 8). ROI is the monetization of a student's amount of learning.

ROI is cobbled together as a prognostication. The jobs and careers that any students will hold during their lifetime and the earnings accumulated from those endeavors are pure unknowns. Jobs and careers that do not exist in the present but will develop in the future confound any meaningful estimation of ROI.

Productivity and Education: The Cost of a Potemkin Village

Russian history provides an instructive example in the twenty-first century of how productivity supplants a focus on teaching and learning in US education. Centuries ago, when one of Russia's czars traveled by boat along the Volga River, local officials built façades of fancy villages along the riverfront.

These fake demonstrations of prosperity—referred to as *Potemkin villages*—fooled the czar into thinking he ruled over a land filled with these villages. Productivity is the Potemkin village in contemporary US education employed to fool parents and caregivers, distract educators, and enthuse policymakers.

Productivity, a façade built out of numbers, speculation, and ideology, represents low-cost teaching and learning sought through free market schooling. Productivity eliminates any need to purchase a student-centric array of instructional programs. Productivity is the low-cost false front mimicking quality teaching and learning. Funding for productivity purchases what amounts to Potemkin education.

Productivity is the impersonation of education. Supposing that cost effectiveness and return on investment are reliable indicators of productivity and imagining that productivity is a valid measure of education is no less foolish than the czar's assumption that his realm was filled with Potemkin villages.

LEGISLATURES: EDUCATION SUPER SHOPPERS IN ACTION

Assuming productivity arises from on-the-cheap funding or the ideology that supports teaching and learning engendered by cost effectiveness and ROI ensures that the bifurcation of US education will continue to afflict teaching and learning. Stuffed with cost effectiveness, ROI, and standardized test data, productivity constitutes an argument for quality education that is neither fact-based nor student-centric (Ford, 2016; Scafidi, 2016).

Productivity: A Legislative Standard Operating Procedure

Across the United States, legislatures have demonstrated a tendency (i) to resist adequate funding for traditional public education; (ii) split or manipulate available resources for schooling; and (iii) adopt inaction as a strategy to ensure that productivity is the "better" funded for education.

Reducing cost and avoiding adequacy, legislatures install productivity as a standard operating procedure (SOP). Reluctance to provide funding necessary for quality teaching and learning throughout all school districts as an SOP means that what taxpayers purchase is often not the schooling they thought they paid for.

Virginia's General Assembly in 2016, for example, "appropriated $339 million less than the resources projected as necessary to deliver the state standards of quality" (Black, 2019, p. 1413). In Washington State, resistance to funding public education took the form of ignoring court-ordered funding reform. Keeping revenue the same, Washington's legislature "refused to respond to court orders for years, eventually forcing the court to impose a $100,000-a-day fine until the state acted" (Black, 2019, p. 1414).

Inaction by New York's legislature on court-ordered funding reform became a drawn-out process lasting several years in the early 2000s. The formula that finally emerged from the legislature, although an incomplete response to a court order, was found to be steps in the right direction sufficient to allow the state court to end its oversight. "In retrospect, all the state had done was promise to adequately fund its schools; [even though] it had not actually done so yet" (Black, 2019, p. 1415).

New Jersey mirrored New York's SOP. After adopting a new funding formula and earning court approval for it, "within two years, the state began grossly underfunding the formula, cutting $1.6 billion from the amount the statutory formula required" (Black, 2019, p. 1415).

BARGAIN-BASEMENT DOLLARS: FOUR EDUCATION PURCHASES

The SOPs of state legislatures are riddled with assumptions about what should be purchased for education and the purchasing power that funding formulas ought to provide. With productivity as a template, legislative assumptions often lead to bargain-basement revenue systems that permit only bargain-basement purchases.

Four purchases are top sellers in this bargain basement: funding system chaos, funding system retrenchment, funding system manipulation, and funding system disconnection. These four funding formula purchases prohibit equity, adequacy, sufficiency, and quality for US public schools. The impersonation of education can be bought at rock bottom prices.

Purchase 1: Funding System Chaos

Chaos ruled state funding formulas during and after the Great Recession of 2008. Across the nation, "more than eighty percent of schools experienced budget cuts." (Jung, 2018, p. 98). "Since 2008, 34 states have cut their K–12 education budgets, and 21 states proposed additional K–12 budget cuts for the 2011–2012 fiscal year" (McNichol, Oliff, and Johnson 2012, as cited in Nelson and Balu, 2014, p. 601).

By purchasing productivity for public schools, ten years after the Great Recession "only a handful of states have returned to pre-recession levels of spending" (Partelow et al., 2018, "Fixing Chronic Disinvestment," para. 2).

Ill-equipped to accommodate significant economic downturns, funding formulas faced fiscal chaos during the coronavirus disease 2019 (COVID-19) pandemic. With tax collections of all kinds in a tailspin beginning in 2020, state leaders faced decisions about public education (e.g., cost, investment) that reinforced the impact of bifurcation.

Funding Chaos on the Coasts

Funding chaos is a purchase that can create dramatic revenue shifts. Several studies in California "found the net loss to school districts for each student who moves from a district to charter school to be somewhere between $3,100 and $6,700" (Lafer, 2018, p. 17). For San Diego's public school system, the "net cost of charter schools in 2016–2017 totaled $65.9 million" (Lafer, 2018, p. 5). Few school districts have the wherewithal to ameliorate this type of funding chaos.

Funding chaos of a different kind is purchased via school funding in Massachusetts. The Bay State's legislature created a built-in structural deficit established "by a revenue base that has been limited by the initiative petition, a reliance on a volatile capital gains tax, and healthcare costs that grow faster than its major revenue sources, the personal income tax and the sales tax" (Snow and Burke, 2019, p. 78).

Efforts by the Massachusetts legislature to lessen the impact of this ongoing deficit aggravated fiscal chaos. Instead of a long-range, permanent fix, legislators drew down rainy day funding, shifted revenue and expenditures, issued fiscal stabilization bonds, and reduced budgets of state agencies (Snow and Burke, 2019). Funding chaos purchased more funding chaos.

Funding Chaos in the Badger State

School choice programs in Wisconsin represent the purchase of another type of funding chaos. An analysis of the funding structure of Milwaukee's voucher program indicated that the state's taxpayers "saved more than $32 million, but Milwaukee's local taxpayers were adversely affected, to the tune of nearly $41 million in fiscal year 2010" (Bruecker, 2017, p. 9).

A dramatic expansion in 2015 of the statewide voucher program in Wisconsin eliminated an existing enrollment cap of one thousand students and initiated a gradual elimination of an enrollment cap on the number of students from each school district who could receive a voucher. Funding chaos for traditional public schools ensued because the Wisconsin legislature's 2015 voucher expansion bill moved the cost of each voucher out of the state's General Purpose Revenue account and made the cost of vouchers the responsibility of local school districts.

By the 2016–2017 school year, in Wisconsin "nearly $23 million was transferred from state equalization aid to school districts to private schools" (Bruecker, 2017, p. 10). With the average voucher amount of $7,214 paid for K–8 students and with the average per-pupil allocation for Wisconsin public school students amounting to $4,545, funding chaos pays for a significant negative impact on learning outcomes (Bruecker, 2017).

Purchase 2: Funding System Retrenchment

State legislators are both super shoppers and finicky shoppers when foundation formulas for public education are involved. Once the US economy was on the mend in the aftermath of the Great Recession of 2008, "many states enacted massive tax cuts that deprived state governments of revenue needed to increase education spending" (Partelow et al., 2018, "States Have Made Deep Cuts," para. 3). Seven states—Arizona, Idaho, Kansas, Michigan, Mississippi, North Carolina, and Oklahoma—making the largest funding cuts in the aftermath of 2008 engaged in cutting taxes instead of reinvesting in schools (Partelow et al., 2018).

Individual state officials also play a role in the retrenchment of public school funding. In New Jersey, for example, after the State Supreme Court ordered the restoration of $13 million that was eliminated from the budget of Trenton schools in 2011–2012, the governor "refused to fund the formula, resulting in an over $41 million shortfall in state aid to TPS [Trenton Public Schools] in 2017–8" (Farrie, 2018, p. 1).

Instead of employing data related to demographics to demonstrate student needs, instead of accessing information about the cost of school professionals who can meet these needs, and instead of engaging with educational experts to determine the level of investment required to deliver dynamic instruction to all students, Ohio's legislature works backward to the number that purchases public education.

In Ohio, "the state does not base the funding formula on any real or objective estimates; it simply fills in the blanks in the formula with numbers that, when multiplied, will equal the preordained amount of money the state is willing to spend" (Black, 2019, p. 1410).

Oregon's approach to retrenchment embraces an easy way out for policymakers wary of raising taxes to pay for public education. This approach is "the so-called 'safety net plan' [that] allowed districts to maintain the previous year's level of local property tax levies without requiring voter approval" (Corcoran et al., 2017, p. 10). But the safety net prohibited new tax levies and, thus, ensured that increased costs in a new school year could not be dealt with except by restricting existing programs.

Avoiding increased funding necessary for uncontrolled costs (e.g., utility rates, insurance costs), this approach puts the burden of less funding on local school districts. Unable to delay, prevent, or negotiate increases in operational expenses, Oregon school districts had less revenue available to sustain and grow instructional programs.

Purchase 3: Funding System Manipulation

The manipulation of funding formulas is a long-standing characteristic of school finance. Some instances of this phenomenon are found in the direct actions of legislators and other public officials.

Literally hiding in plain sight are funding manipulations with a direct impact on teaching and learning. For example, funding siphoned to charter schools created a loss of $25 million annually for traditional public schools in both Durham, North Carolina, and Buffalo, New York, while "in Los Angeles—the nation's second-largest school district—the net loss is estimated at over $500 million per year" (Lafer, 2018, p. 17).

Funding manipulations like these aid and abet the ignominious wages paid to public educators; the declining numbers of graduates emerging from preparation programs in colleges and universities; and the extent to which roles in choice and privatization education tend to be filled by "inexperienced, unqualified, or out of field teachers" (Baker and Weber, 2016, p. 4).

Other instances of funding manipulation are more indirect. Evidence-free assertions promote the need to purchase productivity for bargain-basement traditional public education. The US Department of Education asserted that productivity should be the mainstay of school purchases because educational professionals demonstrated a "lack of effective leadership, lack of comprehensive human capital strategies and otherwise ineffective and inefficient personnel policies" (Baker and Weber, 2016, p. 3).

Purchase 4: Funding System Disconnections

Ostensibly, funding formulas provide public revenue to purchase educational experiences that engage students and expand their natural thinking and lived experience with principled reasoning and skills that maximize life success (Swensson and Shaffer, 2020). Although all learners will not define life success in the same way, all learners deserve a funding system sufficient for and capable of paying for teaching and learning that leads to socially responsible citizenship and life success.

Funding systems disconnect from learners, however, when disparity arises between different school districts. Different funding levels associated with the taxable wealth in different districts allows the disconnection of adequate funding. When scholars contend that funding can be linked to student achievement via school district budgets (Toland, 2016), such an approach is limited when so many funding formulas permit widespread inequity. State legislatures often fail to compensate for this disparity through their own initiative.

Funding is disconnected from student-centric learning. For instance, "students in the fastest-growing segment of private schools, conservative Christian schools, 'are almost a year behind their public school counterparts'" (Levin, 2013, p. 1065).

In Texas, charter schools are not delivering significant improvement of student achievement. Research indicates that "in 2017, nine percent of charters were designated as 'Improvement Required' under the Texas accountability system, compared to only three percent of traditional public schools" (Villanueva, 2019, p. 1).

Disconnections are built-in to funding for education by legislative decision-making. Mandates from legislatures and court decisions that intend to enhance, improve, or fix services designed for disadvantaged youth often are not only unfunded or underfunded but yield significantly increased costs for traditional public schools (Biddle and Berliner, 2002). Stretching existing funding to meet important student needs are funding system disconnections that dilute funding to the disadvantage of all students.

Embedded in funding systems for education, these purchases establish disconnections that are exacerbated by economic and societal factors. For example, funding setbacks during and after the Great Recession of 2008 "reintroduced disparities between rich and poor districts—and have been associated with teacher shortages in poor districts, lower capacity to meet student needs, and concomitant dips in achievement levels and increases in achievement gaps" (Darling-Hammond, 2019, p. 9).

WHO'S MINDING THE STORE?

When it comes to funding public education, the role of each state legislature is to enact the intentions of the state constitution for public education and its funding. The role of the state courts—when the legislature's funding efforts are challenged—is to balance the constitutional language against funding systems and what is paid for in public education.

Legislatures and state courts exercise different degrees of oversight for school funding systems about what is purchased. On the face of things, these two state entities appear to be minding the store where public education is paid for.

Who's minding the store, however, is nothing more than a management façade. Court deference, legislative inaction, or noncompliance are factors more likely than not to be exercised by the governmental entities allegedly minding the public education funding store.

Although the legislative and judicial responsibilities for funding public education are easily identified, disengagement with responsibility is all too common. It turns out that *responsibility-for* can be neglected and *responsibility-to* can be disruptive.

Even when state courts take responsibility and adjudicate funding reform for public education, the courts' decisions are often rendered meaningless. Between 1971 and 2010, "state supreme courts overturned school finance systems in 28 states" (Jackson et al., 2016, p. 162). But when legislatures ignore or bypass rulings like these, oversight evaporates and the funding gaps between low-wealth and high-wealth school districts continue.

Adding insult to injury, minding the store by proxy—when third-person governance executes funding, teaching, and learning—constitutes the "devolution of the responsibility for schooling to the private provision of public services, coupled with the use of public funds to provide that schooling" (Carlson et al., 2013, p. 900).

The Difficulties of Minding the Store

Taking responsibility, minding the store, is "more difficult to achieve when the relevant good or service is highly technical or complex in nature or when desired goals and outcomes cannot be clearly defined or agreed upon by all parties" (Brown and Potoski 2006; Lowery 1998, cited in Carlson et al., p. 900).

Teaching and learning are supremely complex. Oversight of funding for these complexities is a difficulty exacerbated because there is little agreement between the two major perspectives about teaching and learning. Oversight is an almost impossible responsibility because these perspectives are entangled with layers of governance vying for control of purchases linked to the quality of US education.

The extent to which responsibilities are neglected and oversight is an after-thought can be suggested in several examples:

- In Indiana, two virtual schools inflated their enrollments over an eight-year period by fourteen thousand students, which meant that the schools received $68 million in overpayments from the state. This sleight of hand was accomplished by counting students who were receiving no services from these two schools.

  Students were counted and reported to the state after they left the schools and when a parent or caregiver merely called to get information. The taxpayer dollars spirited into the schools' coffers via enrollment fraud were used to pay "millions of dollars to companies where school executives and relatives had a financial stake" (Jackson, 2020).

- In Michigan, despite legislation referred to as Power Equalization Program (PEP) that gave state funding to school districts as a supplement to dollars raised via a local property tax rate, disparate spending between school districts remained.

  The failure of PEP to achieve equalization of funding occurred because (i) local school boards were unwilling to levy taxes at the full PEP rate; (ii) state authorities failed to "enforce uniform fair-market valuations on property throughout the state;" and (iii) full funding of PEP rarely was enacted by the state (Combs et al., 2018, p. 228).

- In Pennsylvania, observers indicate that "Pennsylvania public charter schools have become fraught with 'chicanery and greed . . . excessive executive salaries . . . nepotism, and [dubious] financial and real-estate transactions" (Gallo, 2014, p. 208).

- With the advent of tuition tax-credit contributions, private entities are given the authority to grant so-called "scholarships" that are little more than stealth vouchers sanctioned by legislative action.

  As Baker and Miron (2015) point out, this is "the involvement of an-other private, non-government actor in the flow of funds [that] further limits taxpayer ability to challenge the distribution of tax-related funds" (p. 10). Not only is more funding created in this way for privatization edu-cation but the appearance of less government is also fulfilled despite the fact that bureaucracies must be established to funnel the "contributions" to "scholarships."

The extent to which no one is minding the store for funding US education and the extent to which what's paid for goes unmonitored is illustrated further by a US Government Accountability Office (GAO) report on the oversight available about education savings accounts and voucher programs across the nation. "The information programs have about student characteristics varies and cannot be compared across all programs because of differing data collection methods or definitions for characteristics like race and ethnicity, disability status, and income" (GAO, 2016).

TWO ANSWERS: DOES THE UNITED STATES REALLY PAY FOR THE EDUCATION IT GETS?

Yes and no.

An affirmative answer is based on the relationship between less than sufficient funding and less than adequate learning in too many schools for too many students. Less revenue pays for adult-centric ideologies and prognostications. This "good deal" purchases chaos, disconnection, and inadequacy in education. With little attention given to student-centric quality and with indifferent oversight by governmental entities charged with minding the store, funding pays for the minimum that the United States gets from most public education.

An affirmative answer indicates that the nation has lost sight of the counterproductive dualities that shatter funding and undercut the purchase of quality teaching and learning in public education. The impersonation of education is what society purchases. This purchase does not align with constitutional language. But it does align with less.

Unable to see, understand, and fix the multiple cracks that fragment education, the education the United States purchases has a tangential relationship with what society thought was being purchased. Imagining that education is a purchase that delivers "better" for all students is the equivalent of the czar's self-delusion when he viewed Potemkin villages.

A negative answer to this question emerges when it turns out that the United States pays for neither dynamic instruction nor student-centric instructional programs. A negative answer indicts funding systems for stealing equity and adequacy.

What the United States pays for in education is horribly muddled and adult-centric. Priorities purchased for traditional public education too often are cost focused in pursuit of ideological priorities and other similar expressions of power (Swensson and Shaffer, 2020). Under these circumstances, education and its funding are a test of the expectations and intentions of US society.

Chapter Six

Public Education Is a Test

Public education is a test. Fundamental questions about the nature of a society are answered when education is established and paid for by public initiative. Answering one question—*What is public education?*—tests how a society perceives its core values and the obligations that attend this core. Test answers emerge when legislatures enact preferred educational characteristics, when ideological factors influence how lawmakers and policymakers apply these characteristics, and when public funding follows the factors and characteristics that answer the test.

As any student will relate, few tests are based on one question. The first question a society answers about the nature of education inspires a cascade of related questions. The image a society creates about itself is relayed via answers to questions such as:

- Is education supposed to engage students with *how to think* (e.g., principled reasoning, positive liberty) or with *what to think* (Fraser-Burgess, 2012; Swensson and Shaffer, 2020)?
- What norms and citizenship expectations does education inculcate?
- Is education funded adequately and equitably?
- Does education foster "better" for all students?

Public education, its existence and its funding, is a test of the intentions, goals, meaning, and purpose of a society. Public education tests how the society "sees" itself and what future the society intends for its members.

The purpose of this chapter is to discuss US responses to the test of education. This chapter will explore education and its funding as a test of the expectations, ideals, goals, and intentions for US students and their futures.

Throughout this chapter public education is a test about "better." *"Better"* is introduced as education's roots in the historic disagreement about the role of the public sector in the United States. Divisions created by this fundamental disagreement are aggravated by racism and poverty. These two long-standing failures of US society are examined as significant obstacles to a passing grade on the test of public education.

This discussion details the bifurcation that infests answers to the test of US education. Represented by a back-to-business approach and by assessment riveted to standardized testing, myriad dualities ensure that educational theory and practice are adult-centric. The chapter concludes with dialogue about whether a passing grade is possible on the test of education.

PUBLIC EDUCATION IS A TEST ABOUT "BETTER"

Education is an organized attempt by society at "better." The notion that students are "better" (e.g., readers, thinkers, artists) based on what they learn in schools is well accepted. Public education, also, is supposed to yield the "better" of citizenship and learning about both the government and expectations of a society.

These examples of "better" represent how societies can envision teaching and learning as a function of government and government funding. Such general responses to the test of education do not, however, fully explain how the United States conveys "better" in its answers to the test of education.

"Better" Is Not Always Benign

Societies answer "better" in the test of education to bring a wide range of beliefs and intentions to fruition. These societal visions about "better" are not always benign.

History recounts the malignant "better" answer given by Nazi Germany or the Soviet Union in the test of education. How a society perceives itself and how children are to perpetuate or improve this vision can yield "better" as thinking and actions that exclude, denigrate, and demonize.

Teaching and learning can be used like a cookie cutter to shape students. Imposed in this way, education can be a test strewn with destructive, unjust, practices and outcomes aligned with *what to think* embedded in a society's notions about itself and about "better."

US Answers to the Test of Education

"Better" is evident in the proclamations of both major perspectives about US education. Privatization proponents like Hanushek (2016), for instance, speak to "better" by observing that decades after initial concerns were expressed about the quality of US public education and its influence on learning, "the development of an education system that provides equal educational opportunity for all groups, and especially for racial minorities—has not been attained" (p. 10).

Traditional public education adherents also speak to "better." Improved achievement for all students and the funding necessary for teaching and learning associated with this view of "better" are long-standing goals of traditional public schools. This understanding of "better" is "related to public education—something that has been historically articulated as essential for the development of every individual and society as a whole" (Fitzgerald, 2015, p. 60).

"Better," US History, and the Role of the Public Sector

In response to the test of education, each of the major US perspectives begins with proclamations about "better" but provides divergent answers. US history spotlights one of many fundamental differences between these perspectives rooted in the historical divide in the United States about the role of the public sector in society.

Although the shorthand definition of the public sector's role is "to provide necessary goods and services to the general public" (Jung, 2018, p. 100), little about the US past and present exemplifies such a straightforward understanding.

Long before the invention of US public education in the 1800s, differing views about the role of the public sector in the United States were well-established, waiting as it were to become competing answers on the test of public education in the nation. Dissension over the role of the public sector is embedded in the US response to the test of education and sheds light on the splintered implementation of US teaching and learning.

The Role of the Public Sector: From US Beginnings

From the beginning of the United States, two competing views of the role of the public sector evinced fragmentation of how the nation sees itself. One view of the role of the public sector is represented by the nation's first structure for government, the Articles of Confederation. Disjointed by intent, the first expression of a national public sector was separation expressed as federalism. Fear of central authority—a hangover from the days of King George III—fostered this weak central government. Less government, less public sector, was the nation's first instinct.

Unable to carry out even the most basic roles expected of a national public sector, however, the Articles of Confederation were replaced by the US Constitution. This next attempt at a national public sector was centralized, collaborative, and united. The role of the public sector enshrined in the Constitution continues into the twenty-first century.

As historians illustrate, however, the underlying concepts that give the Constitution and the Articles of Confederation completely different expressions of the role of the public sector continue to divide the nation and its answer to the test of education.

The Public Sector, Public Education, and Bifurcation

The nation's disconnection about the role of the public sector in society is one of many examples of the crevices and cracks that bifurcate public education. Dualities that fragment teaching and learning are reflected in differing views of the role of the public sector. How this dissension plays out in the test of education is illustrated by the different responses to *Brown v. Board* (1954).

On the one hand, fair, collaborative, and just frame one view of "better" in US education envisioned in and after *Brown v. Board* (1954). Studies indicate that some schools that Black students attended at that time received increased revenue and that this response to the landmark ruling by the US Supreme Court was sufficient to reduce class size (Weathers and Sosina, 2019).

Responding to the adjudication of the judicial branch of the federal government, this and other iterations of "better" in the aftermath of *Brown v. Board* "contributed to improved educational attainment, socioeconomic status, and health outcomes for Black students, with no negative impact on White students" (Johnson 2011; Reber 2010, as cited in Weathers and Sosina, 2019, p. 3). Connections and interplay typify the role of the public sector chosen in this response to the test of public education.

On the other hand, states' rights, separation, and singularity are "better" illuminated by a different view of the role of the public sector than that envisioned in *Brown v. Board* (1954). Virginia, for instance, closed all public schools in the wake of this landmark decision (Suitts, 2019). This action and others like it are a legacy of disdain for intervention by the national government. This response embraced the creation and state funding of *segregation academies*; this way of "seeing" society and the role of the public sector exists, excludes, and discriminates in the twenty-first century (Shaffer and Dincher, 2020).

The United States, divided over the role of the public sector, grapples with what is or is not "better" when education is envisioned and paid for by policymakers' answers to the test of education. The bifurcation of the US vision for education and its funding are sketched in several test answers:

- Privatization schools funded with public revenue usually do not have to hire teachers with requisite academic qualifications. "In some states, private school teachers need not even have a bachelor's degree" and only eleven of the states that offer vouchers require that voucher schools be accredited (Weaver, 2018, para. 10).
- "Funding for education is always in competition with the need to provide citizens with other social goods" (Shields et al., 2017, "The Scarcity," para. 1). If "better" is lower taxation, or public goods that have no relationship with education, public schools are unlikely to emerge as a "winner" from this level or type of competition. Legislators and other state officials determine "better" and "winners" when the test of education is reduced to a competition over funding.
- "Justice, if it requires nothing else, requires that governments treat their citizens with equal concern and respect" (Shields et al., 2017, "The State Regulation," para. 2). This broad view of a response to the test of education implies a "better" for education that has significant implications for funding level, effort, and distribution.

Some of these answers replicate the underlying principles of the role for the public sector invoked within the Articles of Confederation: singularity, exclusion, and disconnection of education invoked as a cost and as an individual good. Other answers mirror underlying principles of the Constitution: the common good, social justice, and principled reasoning in education perceived as an investment for the greater good of the public.

FAILING THE TEST BEFORE IT'S GIVEN: POVERTY AND RACISM

Poverty is ever-present in the lives of too many US students and, thus, is omnipresent in US public schools. Racism is embedded in US history and, thus, endemic to the life experience of people of color within the public sector and students of color in the nation's schools.

How the role of the public sector is perceived—either as the primacy of self-aggrandizement or as the construction of the public good—coupled with the ever-present predations visited on students by poverty and racism means that public education can be a test that the US fails before it's given.

Poverty and the Test of US Education

US education has an abiding responsibility for "better" in the lives of all students. The moral obligation of US education is to engage all students with academic proficiencies that facilitate school and life success (Swensson and Shaffer, 2020). Poverty stands in the way of this responsibility and this obligation. US education fails when this formidable obstacle to quality teaching and learning cannot be conquered.

Although education is not the origin of poverty in the United States, education has the capacity to engage students with learning sufficient to eradicate lifelong involvement with poverty. Education fails to address poverty in this way when funding fails to account for the fact that "sixty percent of black and Hispanic students attend majority poor schools, while only 30% of Asian students and only 18% of white students do so" (Orfield and Lee, as cited in Logan and Burdick-Will, 2015, p. 324).

"High rates of student poverty have a significant impact on the levels and types of resources, and the funding needed, to give those students a meaningful opportunity for success in school" (Farrie et al., 2019, p. 12). As early as 2016, more than 50 percent of students enrolled in K–12 public schools were "eligible to receive free or reduced-price lunch" (Suitts, 2016, p. 36).

Economic, social, and other factors in the life experience of students in poverty have a deleterious impact on school success. The negative impact of poverty on learning spawns what scholars refer to as the *income-based achievement gap*. This achievement gap "is now nearly twice as large as the Black–White achievement gap" (Baker et al., 2016, p. 2).

Racism and the Test of US Education

How US society responds to the test of education too often includes overt or covert racism. For example, one state's Education Commissioner opined in the late 1970s, amid litigation to end inequity and inadequacy, that "urban children, even after years of remediation, will not be able to perform in school as well as their suburban counterparts. . . . We are just being honest" (Darling-Hammond, 2019, p. 16).

In too many classrooms, instances of *stereotype threat, marginalization,* and *deficit thinking* stand as contemporary evidence of racist behavior and communications that deny all students the promises and potential of US education (Swensson and Shaffer, 2020).

Racism must be confronted if US society is to deliver on the aspirations of justice and liberty in its historic documents. Racism must be confronted for the United States to have any chance of passing the test presented by education. A long-standing stain on the nation's promises, racism plagues US education (Suitts, 2019; Weathers and Sosina, 2019).

The Destruction of US Teaching and Learning

The failure to address racism and poverty in answers to the test of education accomplishes nothing less than the destruction of teaching and learning. Discriminatory belief systems of those who fund, lead, or teach on behalf of US education "can lead to the argument that because students from impoverished homes are unlikely to benefit from a 'quality' education, funding public schools equally in rich and poor neighborhoods would only waste tax dollars" (Biddle and Berliner, 2002, p. 54).

Bigotry like this exists alongside the fact that "almost all black students attend a school in the top half of the poverty distribution and the lower half of the achievement distribution" (Logan and Burdick-Will, 2015, p. 339). Blaming students and ascribing to them life experience that precludes school and life success are discriminatory and racist actions and attitudes that persist into the twenty-first century.

Among the devastating ideologies at the heart of racism that can influence decision-makers for school funding are

- *Individualism:* This discriminatory perspective "holds that success and failure result mainly from individual effort rather than social circumstance" (Biddle and Berliner, 2002, p. 53).
- *Essentialism:* This ideology ascribes to human beings of color and human beings in poverty inherited "genetic characteristics that account for whatever lack of successes they have experienced" (Biddle and Berliner, 2002, p. 53).

Evoking these ideologies to carry forward the exclusion inherent in racism, voucher and education savings account programs restrict students' enrollment "based on their disability status or family income" (GAO, 2016).

For-Profit and For-Exclusion: Funding Privatization

The failing response of US society to the test of poverty and racism is exemplified in the extent to which public funding for private, for-profit, management of education constitutes an obstacle to both students in poverty and students of color. Answering the test of education with the pursuit of profit is reflected in the tendency of EMOs and other private education entities to choose to operate in locations that maximize revenue.

Lee (2018) points out a way of thinking aligned with the free market about location puts for-profit privatization of education in the same category as the location decisions about shopping malls. "Profit-oriented service vendors, seeking to identify who are financially profitable customers, can make judgments about potential markets on the basis of the demographic and socioeconomic features in a specific place, regardless of service benefits and demands" (p. 5). Locating a privatization school in hopes of maximizing profit is a back-to-business basic of free market theory.

The potential for profit associated with public funding combined with management devoted to maximizing profit accounts for a pattern of charter schools locating near, but not within, areas that are predominantly Black (Gilblom and Sang, 2019). This finding, noted in several studies, represents the financial motivation to locate charter schools where there can be

> access to a steady stream of poor, Black students with less mobility while simultaneously attracting high-ability students of favorable backgrounds who are open to trying a new public school option, specifically students from TPS who require fewer resources to educate and who will most likely enhance the school's performance (Gilblom and Sang, 2019, p. 5).

Hidden in this toxic mix are the intents and effects of marginalized funding for teaching and learning. Hidden are answers to the tests of poverty, racism, and education that exclude students of color and students in poverty. Public education, under these circumstances, is an answer about "better" that fails all students and the promises of democracy.

BACK-TO-BUSINESS: ANSWERING THE TEST OF EDUCATION

Business has never been far removed from US public education. Part of this proximity relates to the fact that in many communities the school district is a major employer. Public schools make large purchases (e.g., food, furniture, energy, cleaning supplies) from businesses, service providers, and industries. The quality of a school system is often a selling point that attracts new economic investment to a community.

Business and education in the United States have another, more complicated, relationship. Schools managed as if they are businesses, sometimes on a for-profit basis, are the heart of this relationship. This relationship provides one answer in the test of education about the nation's values and priorities.

School-as-business intends efficiency, less cost, and competition with other schools. A model for conducting school-as-business accounts for factors (e.g., demographics of a location, the achievement status of nearby schools, the cost of enrolling students living in the location) that allow maximized revenue and reduced cost.

Charter school operators, for example, put a back-to-business to work in "market-oriented charters" (Logan and Burdick-Will, 2015). Market-oriented charters are

- located in areas where home ownership levels are high (Washington, D.C.);
- located near, but not within, low-income areas in which the population is predominantly African American (New Jersey); and
- located in areas where the population is predominately White and high-income (Chicago, Philadelphia, Atlanta) (Koller and Welsch, 2017).

Principles of free market theory guide choice schools to pursue goals that ensure fiscal survival. Full enrollment (a symbol of desirable market share) is a back-to-business priority. The drive to acquire and maintain a viable market share to finance privatization education is inseparable from the mantra of parental choice and competition. Proponents of this business model argue

> that parents have a right to choose schools for their children, that parental choice will lead to a better match between the educational needs and goals of the children and the schools they attend, or that parental choice will put competitive pressure on traditional schools and, thereby, spur them to become better (Ladd, Clotfelter, and Turaeva, 2018, p. 1).

The Component Parts of Privatization Education

When back-to-business is an answer to the test of education, the capabilities and futures of all students are in the hands of schooling that prioritizes "better" for adults: ideologues, policymakers, and legislators. A back-to-business answer to the test of US education activates a signature benefit: adult-centric "better" in the form of an ideological shift. If a principle of free market theory does not suffice as an answer, another back-to-business priority can be substituted without interfering with the intentions of adult-centric education.

For example, improved standardized test scores formerly were the foremost "better" promised by choice education proponents. But this "better" evaporated when privatization education led to no significant academic difference for students: "rigorous research, from groups like Mathematica

Policy Research and Stanford University, has found that average charter performance is roughly equivalent to that of traditional public schools" (Sass, Zimmer, Gill, and Booker, 2016; Schneider, 2019, para. 13).

The next "better" answer to the test of education is substituted by privatization education advocates. "Nontest score outcomes such as high school graduation, college enrollment, and persistence, and earnings may be of greater consequence than test scores" (Sass et al., 2016, p. 684). Like a malfunctioning component part, standardized testing is removed and different free market priorities become viable test responses.

Similar shifts are exercised by ultrawealthy proponents of privatization education. When the small-schools initiative funded by the Gates Foundation (a little more than $51 million given to New York City public schools to transform twelve high schools into sixty-seven small schools) did not achieve anticipated results, "Gates turned his attention to charter schools" (Rogers, 2015, p. 752). Whack-a-Mole philanthropy became a business model for school reform.

The unfulfilled promise of academic improvement once embedded in the ideology of free market schooling was jettisoned in favor of replacement exemplars of "better." Failure to deliver a priority of free market theory, despite what it suggests about the impact of privatization education on learning, leads to ideological substitution that sustains adult-centric answers to the test of US education. The ease of applying *accountability-to* in choice education facilitates any ideological shift.

NEVER "BETTER" STANDARDIZED TESTING

Assessment, in the form of standardized testing, has come to dominate US education. Standardized tests are touted as an efficient means to measure productivity. Hanushek (2020) opines that "most people recognize that the common achievement tests measure skills that are important for the individual when in the labor market" (p. 5).

To assert that standardized testing offers tea leaves that not only measure the skills important in the labor market of the present but also foretells the skills required for the labor market of the future is a fundamental misunderstanding of standardized testing. Moreover, as studies indicate, "student achievement on tests accounts for just 20% of the effects of educational attainment on earnings" (Bowles, Gintis, & Osborne, 2001, as cited in Shields et al., 2017, "Equality of Educational Opportunity," para. 3).

The fantasy that standardized testing results foretell a student's economic future may be related to misguided notions about the content and intellectual rigor of these assessments. Choice education proponents assert, for instance, that "cognitive development is the nurturing of intellectual ability and knowledge in students that we expect schools to support, commonly measured by standardized tests" (Wolf et al., 2014, p. 14).

The skills required for future employment success seem unlikely to have a strong relationship with fill-in-the-blank, lower-order cognition, short-answer, or formulaic writing required for success on a standardized test. In addition, standardized tests are devoid of the so-called soft skills (e.g., tenacity, resilience, empathy) that are omnipresent in the must-have skills of employees sought by business and industry in the twenty-first century (Shields et al., 2017).

Always ready to replace a component part, some privatization education advocates recognize that standardized tests measure limited cognitive skills in limited subject areas (e.g., mathematics, reading, language arts) and, thus, are not nearly adequate to an assessment of the full impact of public education. Shifting once again, these advocates note that "test scores are merely an intermediate outcome of education" (Wolf et al., 2014, p. 21).

The failure of privatization education to deliver consistently better results on standardized tests than traditional public schools calls into question the viability of any comparison that pretends productivity is "better" that answers the test of education.

Testing: The Anchor for Public Funding

An easy-come-easy-go approach to standardized testing suggests that advocates of privatization education are more in search of a rationale for ideological supremacy than a test answer with a meaningful impact on teaching, learning, and the future of US democracy. But comments about tossing aside standardized testing do not preclude privatization proponents promoting test results and test comparisons.

Standardized testing, from the perspective of privatization advocates, functions as evidence that funding for traditional public education is money poorly spent. For instance, privatization proponents asserted at one point that "we have to make the simplifying assumption that all revenues received by schools in FY11 contributed to math and reading achievement with half supporting math and half supporting reading" (Wolf et al., 2014, p. 15).

The logical and practical absurdity of this assumption notwithstanding, anchoring funding to testing results is a prime opportunity to decry overspending on traditional public education and demand that this cost be curtailed. The disconnection between testing results and higher-order achievement matters little when less cost is an answer to the test of education that legislatures expect.

Anchoring revenue to test results also promotes less cost when critics of traditional public education insist that educators' salaries should be tied to student academic performance (Hanushek, 2020). Assuming student proficiency on standardized tests is the ultimate measure of good teaching is little more than an ideological fantasy.

Another consequence of anchoring funding and salaries to test results is the restriction of instructional practices to what's known as test prep (Swensson and Shaffer, 2020). Test prep necessitates a curriculum devoid of subjects like art, music, and industrial technology, which means fewer teachers are needed and less cost is the achievement.

The negative sanctions—that is, wholesale changes for schools judged by low test results—associated with standardized testing results constitute a cost for students. Teachers limit their instruction to test prep about state standards that are likely to be tested and to skills required to successfully navigate the nuances inherent in the process of taking a standardized test.

Of abiding concern is the cost of this rote learning to students in "schools of a low socio-economic status (SES) [who] have less access to subject areas outside the core subjects than students from high SES schools" (Manzo, 1996; 2005; Pinzur, 2004; von Zastrow and Janc, 2004, as cited in King and Zucker, 2005, p. 6). Not only are answers to the test of education anchored to standardized assessment, but this anchor can be manipulated.

The most blatant example of this manipulation occurred when states and the federal government colluded during the implementation of NCLB to fashion cut scores and standards to allow schools to claim standardized testing success. The gist of this effort was nothing less than relaxing "proficiency requirements in order to help schools and districts avoid failing AYP" (Kogan, Lavertu, and Peskowitz, 2016, p. 422).

Proponents of standardized testing invest test results with the capacity for demonstrating the worth and adequacy of schools and school districts. But the myriad flaws associated with using these assessments as accountability measures are compounded when proficiency rates are set by a state to determine whether test results indicate quality or lack of quality in a school or school district.

In the first place, proficiency rates are subject to manipulation and proficiency rates "largely capture the aptitude students possess *prior* to entering school" (see Downey, von Hippel, and Hughes 2008, as cited in Kogan et al., 2016, p. 422). In the second place, predetermined numbers that represented AYP, or any other similar absolute determination of student proficiency, "only partially (if at all) reflected the effectiveness of their teachers or the quality of their schools" (Kogan et al., 2016, p. 423).

The annual cost of standardized testing—estimated in 2019 at $1.7 billion (Penn State, 2019)—is a dubious expenditure. The value of standardized thinking demanded by these expensive assessments is decreasing as significant numbers of colleges and universities abandon reliance on SAT and ACT assessments, the cousins of K–12 standardized testing, while paying no attention to K–12 standardized test results for any student.

A PASSING GRADE ON THE TEST OF EDUCATION?

Earning a passing grade on the test of education is an objective fraught with uncertainty. Fragmented, education and funding for education cannot escape the inequity, inadequacy, and discrimination visited on students throughout the United States by racism and poverty.

According to 2019 data shared by the NCES, 18 percent of students in public school live in poverty, 26 percent are near-poor, and 56 percent are nonpoor. This same data reveals that 8 percent of students in private schools live in poverty, 13 percent are near-poor, and 79 percent are nonpoor (Feuerstein and Henry, 2020).

Why Earning a Passing Grade Is Difficult

The role of public education is subject to division. Dualities, bifurcation, throughout US schooling impede school funding and school practices necessary to engage all students with substantive learning for their evolving futures. Several divisions stand in the way of student-centric answers to the test of education:

- *Accountability:* Accountability is an answer to the test of education divided between *accountable-for* and *accountable-to.* The damage done by this split is suggested by an aspect of federal legislation, the NCLB. *Accountable-to* at the core of this act was referred to as AYP.

  Anchored to free market theory, AYP, was "based in large part on arbitrary, changing, or politically determined benchmarks that varied across states and within states over time" (Kogan et al., 2016, p. 423). *Accountable-to* established AYP but could not deliver academic proficiency; *accountable-for* reacted to AYP with test prep without engaging all students with quality teaching and learning.
- *Resource limitation:* The bifurcation fostered by the two major perspectives about US education is a function of the difference between cost and investment. During the first sixteen years of the twenty-first century, "the

nation's per-pupil expenditure (adjusted for inflation) in public schools increased by barely more than 14 percent—less than half the rate of growth in the numbers of poor students" (Suitts, 2016, p. 37).

- *Ideological preference:* Latching on to one major perspective about US education or the other puts policymakers and legislators beside a chasm. On one side of the divide is a state's constitutionally enacted traditional public education. On the other side is schooling preference for malleable ideology. The Cleveland Scholarship Program illustrates the ease with which the sides of the chasm grow apart.

    Initially, "no more than 50 percent of recipients may have been previously enrolled in a private school (Ohio Rev. Code 3313.975(B), 1995, amended 2015)" (Stewart and Moon, 2016b, p. 2). When this preference no longer served ideology, Ohio's budget bill for the 2016–2017 biennium eliminated the enrollment requirement. Ideological preference gives rise to an additional discriminatory duality: *enrollment eligible* and *enrollment restricted.*

    Restricted enrollment throughout privatization education limits the resource of learning to chosen students. Eligibility of all students for enrollment in traditional public education stretches limited funding resources when choice schools close or when these schools exclude students.

- *Whose "Better" Is Better?* "Every state constitution guarantees the right to receive an education with variations regarding whether there is also some guarantee regarding the quality of the education states are expected to provide" (Atchison, 2019, p. 3). How a state enacts constitutional guarantees to answer the test of education is how iterations of "better" can misdirect funding, instruction, and learning.

- *Let the Buyer Beware:* Free market theory warrants mechanisms (e.g., charter schools, vouchers, tax scholarships), efficiency, and competition as teaching and learning. Although there is little if any research that validates any of these as reliable or valid precursors for, or progenitors of, quality teaching or robust learning, ideologues, policymakers, and political leaders persist in funding these unproductive, unproven, and unreliable purchases offered in the free market.

Why Earning a Passing Grade Is Possible

The extent to which it is possible to earn a passing grade on the test of education depends on funding sufficient to enhance the capabilities of all students while contributing to the long-term elimination of the national disgrace of persistent poverty and racism. Studies shed light on this possibility:

- The income achievement gap is not so great as to be immune to funding intervention. Jackson et al. (2016) found "that a 25% increase in per pupil spending throughout the school-age years could eliminate the attainment gaps between children from low-income and nonpoor families" (p. 214).

- "In order to strive for more equitable student outcomes, there in fact should be a positive—progressive—correlation between aggregate resources allocated and factors such as child poverty concentrations, disability concentrations and language barriers" (Baker and Green, 2014, as cited in Baker and Weber, 2016, p. 7).
- "For children from low-income families, increasing per pupil spending yields large improvements in educational attainment, wages, family income, and reductions in the annual incidence of adult poverty" (Jackson et al., 2016, p. 212).

Expectations that bifurcate, discriminate, isolate, and deconstruct the student-centric possibilities of language about education in state constitutions constitute failing answers on the test of public education. A passing grade depends on closing gaps that deny the ideals within the nation's founding documents and historic aspirations. A passing grade results from answers to education's test that equip all students with capacities for fairness, respect, social justice, and positive liberty.

Capacities that all US students deserve from engaging with public education include:

- Information derived from subject-area disciplines;
- developing memory to store and retrieve information;
- *how to think* that interconnects information, memory, prior experience, and new knowledge (Swensson et al., 2019b).

All represent the creative, behavioral, and cognitive "better" that is possible when the original power of education and dynamic instruction suffuse the role of US schools (Swensson and Shaffer, 2020). If "better" is invoked without an instructional focus and the funding sufficient to this end, however, "better" is fractured by opposing views in the United States about the role of the public sector.

A STUDY GUIDE FOR THE TEST
THE UNITED STATES CANNOT FAIL

A passing grade on any test frequently aligns with the extent to which a study guide is used. Although a study guide neither provides the questions nor gives the answers to a test, a study guide orients test takers to the expectations to be met if a passing grade is to be earned. Given the test of public education, the state of Connecticut provides a valuable example of the study guide for the test the United States cannot fail.

Jump-started by a 1977 decision of the State Supreme Court, Connecticut began a decade-long journey to improve the quality of teaching and bring equal opportunity to the state's students.

In 1986, an omnibus bill titled the Education Enhancement Act "coupled major increases in teacher salaries with higher standards for teacher education and licensing, and substantial investments in mentoring for beginning teachers and professional development for all staff" (Darling-Hammond, 2019, p. 9).

Connecticut took aim at disparities among school districts through a focus on low-wealth districts and the need for resources to improve instruction in those localities. By 1986, NAEP results for fourth graders in both reading and math put Connecticut first in the nation. Reading and writing proficiency for eighth graders, at the same time, rose to first in the nation while Connecticut's students were outperformed in science in the world only by Singapore (Darling-Hammond, 2019).

Choosing "Better" Answers

The lesson affirmed by Connecticut's example is that funding is critical to adequate teaching and learning. Research that projects the adequacy of spending required for the highest poverty school districts in each state to reach the national average on standardized testing demonstrates that the majority of states' funding is insufficient to teaching and learning worthy of the promises made to all students about education.

The predictions shared in this research reveal that thirty-four states provide less than 80 percent of the funding necessary for high-poverty districts to reach this goal (Baker et al., 2019).

"In most states, the resources expended by the highest-poverty districts are well below what would be required for these students to perform at average levels, and in some states, actual spending is but a small fraction of the estimated requirement" (Baker et al., 2019, p. 13). The extent of the inadequacy and inequity of answers to the test of education is revealed when so many states do not fund schools sufficiently to permit students learning experiences that foster success on the nation's misguided and lower-order standardized tests.

Chapter Seven

The Magic and the Consequences of School Funding

Magic shows and consequences go together. Magicians offer illusions intended to fool and delight audiences. Audiences attend magic shows to be dazzled by sleight of hand and consequences intended by the magician. Magicians present their illusions knowing that the audience expects to be fooled. At some level, magicians and their audiences collude over consequences with no one the worse for wear.

Although state legislators are not magicians by trade, school funding machinations can be mistaken for a show overflowing with illusions. If this is magic, however, the audience and the magicians do not always share the same expectations. What legislators and state officials want their audiences to see and what the audiences expect when sleight of hand and school funding combine can produce a befuddling blend of intentional and unintentional consequences.

The purpose of this chapter is to discuss the consequences of the unique magic practiced across the nation when state legislators perform the school funding show. This discussion begins with the tricks of the trade in the magic of school funding. The school funding show is described in terms of what the audience sees compared to what the audience gets.

Among the consequences of sleight of hand practiced at the fifty statehouses are *intentional impermanence*, *education as a commodity*, and *virtual education as real profit*. The relevance of two aphorisms as consequences of statehouse prestidigitation is discussed. Three dire consequences of the school funding show, alongside what it might take to re-fund public education beyond illusion, conclude the chapter.

STATEHOUSE MAGICIANS AND
THE SCHOOL FUNDING SHOW

Magicians rely on deception and distraction. These tools of the trade have been on stage with magicians for centuries. From no less a stage than the legislatures of the fifty states are these talents spotlighted. When funding for public education is part of the legislative school funding show, dazzling displays of legerdemain are the order of the day.

Prestidigitation in the statehouse transforms the language in state constitutions about public education. Magic tricks divide school funding and, at times, make it disappear. Policies and statutes replace *hocus pocus* as a magic incantation.

The art of misdirection is a magician's best friend. Statehouse magicians embrace this friendship. For example, in one hand, legislators may offer the intentions and outcomes associated with funding traditional public education. In the other hand, unnoticed, legislators hold the intended magic: funding for privatization. Successfully executed, magic at the statehouse obscures funding totals, funding results, and funding answers to the test of education.

Magic Show Expectations

Audiences who attend a magician's performance expect to be fooled; that's part of the fun. But public expectations about public education and its funding evince little tolerance for trickery. Legislators, when all is said and done, are counted on to generate "an equal and quality education to all students" (Black, 2019, p. 1422).

The extent to which a legislature engages in educational gerrymandering denies the fulfillment of this expectation. Legislative sleight of hand is omnipresent. A basic bit of legislative magic occurs when education is perceived as a cost. The motives of states for "intentionally keeping the multiplier for low-income students low or non-existent is not to provide an appropriate level of funding or to ensure efficiency in educational expenditures. It is to arbitrarily reduce the amount the state spends on these students" (Black, 2019, p. 1416).

Pulling an intention to underfund education out of the funding hat is a common trick. Texas, for instance, "explicitly capped the number of special education students it would serve and incentivized districts to do the same. In doing so it created a $3.2 billion funding gap for special education students within just a few years" (Black, 2019, p. 1417).

Alabama's version of intentional underfunding provides each school district with "an added 2.5 weight for 5% of their total population, even though every system has more than 5% of the population identified as special needs" (ALSDE, 2015, as cited in Larkin, 2016, p. 18).

Other types of funding magic share now-you-see-it-now-you-don't. Georgia made $112 million designed to reduce the gap between low-wealth and high-wealth districts disappear from the state's formula; in Illinois, school districts with high numbers of students in poverty stopped receiving state funding for Advanced Placement courses; and both Vermont and New Hampshire declined to fund public education in areas where student needs are greatest despite having the fiscal wherewithal to do so (Black, 2019).

Odd tricks can appear during a school funding show to help costs disappear. For example, Alabama legislators use a ratio of students to leaders to determine for each school "the number of school leaders including principal, assistant principal, counselors, and career tech directors" (Larkin, 2016, p. 18).

The Show Must Go On

There are times when a magician's misdirection and sleight of hand do not fool an audience. A legislature's tricks during the school funding show can be unmasked when brought before state courts.

As a case in point, Kentucky's funding formula was called out by a decision from the state's Supreme Court. *Rose v. Council for Better Education* "held that the state had failed in its duty to 'provide for an efficient system of common schools'" (Combs et al., 2018, p. 229).

After this trick was detected, the legislature responded with the Kentucky Education Reform Act (KERA). KERA was passed by the legislature to redress the consequences of disastrous magic that provided inequitable resources for low-poverty and high-poverty school districts.

KERA, however, proved to be nothing less than a different trick with a result identical to the magic undone by the courts. After KERA became law, researchers looked at the impact of an increase in home value per pupil on the revenue per-pupil in school districts with differing property wealth. This study found that "the gap in wealth effects on combined state-local resources is larger in magnitude at the end of the panel than it was prior to KERA" (Combs et al., 2018, p. 241).

What You See Is Not What You Get

Legislative magic frequently ensures that what the public sees in legislation is not what the public gets. This phenomenon frequently goes unnoticed. But if a legislator reveals that some feature of legislation is an "unintended consequence," what was unintended frequently lies at the center of the magician's trick.

Indiana's voucher program, for example, was held up in one hand by the legislature and other state officials as funding for students who had attended traditional public schools previously but wanted to transfer to a better, private school. Hidden in the other hand of the General Assembly, however, were magically different funding consequences. Appearing out of thin air, legislation allowed "spending money in addition to the voucher amounts that follow public school students to private schools by paying for the tuition of students who had previously been paying out of pocket or receiving a private scholarship" (Moon and Stewart, 2016, p. 8).

THE CONSEQUENCE OF INTENTIONAL IMPERMANENCE

Public institutions—depending on how the role of the public sector is implemented—have the potential to establish permanence of the common good. The utility and worth of common goods like libraries, fire departments, or water works relieve individuals of the need to create personal iterations of these goods. At the same time, common goods are an investment in shared cost. The intentional permanence of public institutions in US democracy establishes networks through which the promises of equality, justice, fairness, and the social contract can be pursued (Swensson and Shaffer, 2020).

Taxes constitute permanent funding for public institutions. Established by duly constituted representative authorities (e.g., city councils, school boards, state legislatures), taxes have the potential to sustain and improve the institutions and networks of democracy. But with the advent of what some scholars refer to as *new public management* (Ford, 2016), funding for public institutions and the status of public education allows common goods to become impermanent.

Free market theory and the provision of government services by nongovernmental entities lie at the foundation of new public management. These foundational elements are illustrated by the Milwaukee Parental Choice Program (MPCP) which "was designed to increase productivity [compared to traditional public schools] by obtaining similar or increased educational outcomes for students for substantially less taxpayer support" (Ford, 2016, p. 883).

New public management envisions a dramatic restructuring of the role of permanent institutions such as public education. As one wealthy proponent of privatization education asserts, the "data show the greatest positive outcomes for students happen when entire school systems are either redesigned or started anew" (Broad 2012a: 143, as cited in Rogers, 2015, p. 743).

The Rise of Impermanence

The role of the public sector hearkens back to the days of the Articles of Confederation when policymakers and lawmakers establish the intentional impermanence of public services facilitated by a competitive market. "A number of local and state governments in the US have transferred activities and functions from public spheres to private organizations" (Lee, 2018, p. 4). Because markets are amoral (Lubienski, 2013), competition for public dollars, market share, and ideological purity engender impermanence.

Impermanence is an intention of free market theory. Choice schools close their doors if they cannot compete successfully against other schools for enrollment and, thus, for funding. Gilblom and Sang (2019) found that charter schools in Ohio's largest urban areas with high percentages of Black students enrolled are most likely to close. "Our findings suggest that the most vulnerable populations in OBEUC [Ohio's 'Big 8' Urban Counties] are exposed to unstable educational institutions that are not providing the innovation and improved outcomes on which TCS [traditional charter schools] are predicated" (Gilblom and Sang, 2019, p. 26).

The Permanence of Impermanence

Impermanence is a consequence with an intensely personal effect. The sixty-two voucher programs in twenty-nine states (as of 2019) "provide public funding to schools that can legally remove or refuse to serve certain students altogether" (Fiddiman and Yin, 2019, "The Danger," para. 1).

Ultimately, adherents of choice education envision permanence of this impermanence. Leading the way to this result are venture philanthropists who sink hundreds of millions of dollars into privatization schools and into third-party entities that advocate for these schools.

Venture philanthropists perceive their donations as educational reform undertaken "with the express intent of changing how things are done that will ultimately be funded by taxpayers" (Rogers, 2015, p. 748). This version of a marketplace for education relishes the competition that ensconces impermanence in the name of free market theory but that will be guaranteed by the permanence of public funding.

THE CONSEQUENCE OF EDUCATION AS A COMMODITY

Lee (2018) describes the descent of US public education from common good to the impermanence of *commodity*. Commodities are primary agricultural products or raw materials (e.g., coffee, corn, copper). Reducing education to the status of a commodity means that a host of back-to-business assumptions can be applied. Foremost among these assumptions is that education, like any other commodity, is a source of profit if costs are kept low and risks are reduced.

As is the case with any commodity, competition among vendors and entities renders profit a function of risk. When it's considered to be a commodity, education is reduced to a bottom-line riveted to fiscal success. In the marketplace, the value of a commodity is enhanced by manipulation of supply and demand. When competition over a commodity overtakes the role of education, the consequences are adult-centric visions of teaching and learning.

"Charter schools in competitive markets protect their market position by opting for less costly and more easily educated students, and by excluding students from low-income or single-parent families" (Lee, 2018, p. 13).

Profit can be squeezed out of pure implementation of free market schooling because "private voucher schools can discriminate against students based on their religion, LGBT status, disability, academic achievement, and disciplinary history" (Weaver, 2018, para. 10).

Consequences following in the wake of marketplace education—segregation, depletion of funding for traditional public schools, lackluster student academic performance—illustrate that entrepreneurs want little to do with costs that do not "fit" the business plan. Funding requirements for quality learning and teaching also take a back seat to efficiency, profit, and ideological "victory." Shaping the commodity means the consequences of the free market put US education in the grasp of avarice.

Buying and Selling in the Educational Marketplace

Buying and selling education as a commodity is a business practice eagerly undertaken by large companies. For example, in the second decade of the twenty-first century the not-for-profit Pearson Foundation (now a defunct entity) developed teaching materials aligned with the Common Core State Standards (CCSS).

After completing work on these materials, the foundation was faced with legal action initiated by the New York Attorney General's Office. The lawsuit accused the foundation of violating prohibitions against using charitable assets to bring financial gain to a for-profit parent company (known, at the time, as Pearson Education). The foundation settled the lawsuit for almost $8 million.

After the settlement, "the Pearson parent company [later known as Savvas] then bought the already developed materials for a reported $15 million" (Rogers, 2015, p. 750).

The almost $23 million expended is an insignificant sum compared to the profit Pearson Education anticipated from selling the CCSS-aligned materials. Treating public education as a commodity, large companies buy and sell teaching and learning as if they are so many pork bellies. Education as a commodity yields rewards from the marketplace tied to free market theory that supplant student-centric outcomes.

THE CONSEQUENCE OF VIRTUAL EDUCATION AS REAL PROFIT

Futures options are bought and sold on *futures contracts*, which are agreements on a fixed price for a commodity but the agreed-on cost does not have to be paid immediately.

Futures options allow entrepreneurs to profit from savvy buying and selling during which no actual items, goods, or services are exchanged. In the same way, virtual or online education provides entrepreneurs with sizeable profit from education when, in many cases, little actual teaching and learning occur.

Two for-profit EMOs—K–12 Inc. and Connections Academy—account for almost 30 percent of the nation's virtual school enrollment.

Direct Profit and Indirect Profit

Not only do EMOs seek to maximize profit by managing privatization schools (e.g., virtual schools, charter schools), but there is profit to be made when EMOs establish what Molnar et al. (2019) refer to as a *vendor relationship*. EMOs can provide products or services to choice schools as an additional pathway to profit.

Largesse, if not strictly profit, arises when choice schools are given more money than the actual cost of educating enrolled students. In Pennsylvania, for example, charter schools receive "tuition payments for a local school district's costs rather than the charter schools actual costs" (Gallo, 2014, p. 217).

Supply and demand play a role in profit acquired when education is a commodity. As has been discussed previously, privatization schools tend to locate where profit can be maximized based on the demographics of an area. The success of choice schools as a commodity also depends on manipulating enrollment so that more valuable commodities—students whose attendance does not involve substantial cost—attend.

This consequence prompted a blunt observation from a charter advocate: "We've turned education into a commodity—if that kid walks across the street, you're chasing after him for the money attached to his seat" (Schneider, 2019).

Limiting overall enrollment ensures that the market share of a given choice school is robust but not so sizeable as to drive down profit. Enrollment limitations are cost effective because, for instance, "the more voucher students a school takes on, the greater the negative impact on students' academic performance" (Weaver, 2018, para. 9).

If Education Is a Commodity, Educators Are, Too

Salaries and benefits are 80–90 percent of the cost of education. Purchasing education as a commodity at the lowest possible price, then, entails reducing the "purchase price" of educators. The extent to which educators have become a commodity sought at the lowest possible price is suggested by data from 2018 that indicated that "teachers are earning almost 2 percent less than they did in 1999 and 5 percent less than their 2009 pay, according to the U.S. Department of Education" (Picchi, 2018, p. 1).

The price of educators as a commodity can be tallied by comparing average starting salaries for teachers and college graduates in other fields. The average starting salary for a teacher in 2018 was $38,617. "The average salary for recent college grads overall is about $50,400" (Picchi, 2018, p. 2).

Under these circumstances, the "purchase price" of a starting teacher has a dramatic effect on supply and demand. Unlike copper, sugar, or other commodities, teachers respond to this purchase price and, thus, influence supply. As Picchi (2018) indicates, "an increasing number of teachers [are] leaving the field for jobs in other industries" (p. 2). Teacher shortages are a commodity shortage that legislators and policy-makers are loath to address substantively when low cost education is a priority.

Teacher shortages correspond with the purchase of low-cost commodities. Bargain-basement funding that treats educators as commodities also prompts "the conclusion that both teachers' overall wages and relative wages affect the quality of those who choose to enter the teaching profession, and whether they stay once they get in" (Baker and Weber, 2016, p. 9).

Consequences tend to pile up in a market. Manipulations and mechanisms associated with privatization education do not guarantee satisfied customers. The expansion of charter schools in several cities, for instance, led to unpopular consequences including "the loss of neighborhood schools and the jobs that go with them, the turmoil of school closures, and the demise of political influence that follows in privatization's wake" (Berkshire, 2019, para. 14).

THE INSPIRING APHORISMS OF FREE MARKET FUNDING

Funding is a sizeable consequence of the language about education in state constitutions. "From school year 2014–15 to school year 2015–16, total revenues for public schools increased by $27 billion (4 percent), from $679 billion to $706 billion in constant 2017–18 dollars" (McFarland et al., 2019, p. 137).

Hundreds of billions of dollars spent on a commodity each year present companies and entrepreneurs with opportunities. Financial stakes of this magnitude are alluring to the point that two aphorisms come to mind: *to the victor belong the spoils* and *money is the root of all evil*. These two sayings are symbolic of the present and future if the role of the public sector is to disburse revenue to third parties that operationalize free market principles.

Money Is the Root of All Evil

If, as the saying goes, money is the root of all evil, then the combination of massive amounts of public funding and limited oversight of this revenue is a circumstance tailor-made for trouble. Evidence of the undesirable potential in this combination emerged from an investigation of virtual academies operated by K–12 Inc.

Conducted by the California Attorney General, this investigation mirrored parallel investigations that identified a "lack of adequate accountability structures linked to how virtual schools account for instructional seat time and report student enrollment, which are used to calculate local and state funding for virtual school students" (Molnar et al., 2019, "Eliminating Profiteering," para. 2).

Findings by the Attorney General of California led to a legal settlement in which K–12 Inc. returned almost $2 million in taxpayer funding to the state. In Ohio, an audit of the state's largest virtual school found that enrollment was over-reported by nine thousand students. This finding led to the Ohio Department of Education seeking a return of $83 million from the school, known as the Electronic Classroom of Tomorrow (Molnar et al., 2019).

"Better," in these and other cases across the nation, is a back-to-business bottom line. This line represents economic advantage instead of academic proficiency. Buying and selling a commodity involves risks; profit or loss are a part of trading in commodities like sugar or copper. The business advantages of treating education like a commodity is that profit is guaranteed by taxation while risks of all kinds are transferred to learners, educators, and the public.

To the Victor Belong the Spoils

Winning is a primary objective when profit and ideology are the inspirations for schooling. When winning combines with minimal regulation or oversight, the self-aggrandizing core of free market theory encourages a winner-take-all approach. When a marketplace victor decides there are spoils to be had from a commodity paid for by public funding, few restraints prevent fiscal malfeasance.

In Florida, for example, companies owned by a businessman managed fifteen charter schools. Of the $57 million in public funding received by these charter schools between 2007 and 2016, more than $1 million were used by the businessman "for personal expenses and to purchase residential and business properties in Florida" (Wright, 2017).

The same businessman used "more than $3.2 million, to buy furniture, computers, equipment and services at grossly marked-up prices" from vendors affiliated with him and his companies (Wright, 2017).

In Pennsylvania, the founder of a charter school "was charged with defrauding three charter schools of more than $6.5 million between 2007 and April of 2011" (Gallo, 2014, p. 225). Pennsylvania's story of privatization school funding is a nightmarish tale playing out at the expense of the common good. "All in all, according to Pennsylvania's Auditor General, Pennsylvania taxpayers are being overcharged $365 million annually as a result of Pennsylvania's charter school funding scheme" (Gallo, 2014, p. 226).

In Los Angeles, the founder and CEO of a charter school operator was sentenced to thirty months in federal prison after pleading guilty to misappropriating and embezzling public funds. In this instance, between 2009 and 2017 the CEO and co-conspirators falsely certified that their charter schools complied with all rules regarding expenses made with public monies. The expenses in this case fraudulently certified as proper:

> included unauthorized first-class airfare and foreign travel, luxury items purchased from shops in Beverly Hills and Tokyo, expensive meals at high-end restaurants, airfare and lodging for herself, her family members, and others in January 2013 to attend President Barak Obama's second inauguration (States News Service, 2019).

Across the United States, the two most reported reasons for charter closure are financial or mismanagement. Almost 42 percent of charter closures are due to financial causes, while an additional 24 percent of charter closures are "due to administrator or sponsor misbehavior" (Consoletti, 2011, as cited in Gilblom and Sang, 2019, p. 4).

When free market education proponents set their sights on education as a profit center, expectations can be galvanized to the adult-centric "side" of the dualities that split US education. The intentional impermanence fostered by competition in the educational marketplace is articulated by venture philanthropist Eli Broad, who explained that "we don't simply write checks to charities. Instead we practice 'venture philanthropy.' And we expect a return on our investment" (Broad Foundation 2012, as cited in Rogers, 2015, p. 756).

SCHOOL FUNDING: DIRE CONSEQUENCES

Public education and its funding are subject to interpretation. Whether the authors of language in state constitutions about education intended this ambiguity, history's verdict is that interpretation and consequences arising from interpretation are the centerpiece of each state's consequences for schools and school funding. Among the consequences with dire impacts on US teaching and learning are (i) *legislative supremacy*, (ii) *funding misdirection*, and (iii) *obstruction of the common good*.

Consequence: Legislative Supremacy

Legislatures respond to judicial rulings about inequitable funding with magic tricks that delay these rulings or restore the intentions of the original legislation. Legislatures manage to exercise their own oversight and impose their own consequences; legislative supremacy skirts the functionality of the checks and balances in democracy.

Overturning Court Rulings

Legislative supremacy is exercised when legislators delay or impede court rulings that require substantive alteration of existing school funding formulas. As Atkinson (2019) observes, "not all court cases that overturn the state system of school funding lead to meaningful changes in the education finance system" (p. 3).

State court rulings in New York, for example, found that changes were required in the funding formula to end inequitable distribution of educational resources. As New York's legislature slowly worked on a fix, the Great Recession of 2008 hit. Instead of continuing to work to abide by the court's order for funding reform, the state froze and then cut aid to public schools.

These freezes and cuts led to high-wealth districts increasing local funding effort while the state facilitated property tax relief for the school districts with the lowest percentages of students in poverty. "The resulting effect was a system of school funding which remained regressive and maintained large funding discrepancies between districts" (Atkinson, 2019, p. 6). Hamstrung when legislatures ignore or defy rulings, state courts have little recourse to remedy recalcitrant legislative responses.

Judicial Deference

The state of Illinois offers a prime example of legislative supremacy aided and abetted by judicial deference. Historically, Illinois has relied on local sources for funding public education to the extent that state aid contributes about 30 percent, federal aid contributes 10 percent, and "local school districts provide on average almost sixty percent of the funding on which they [public schools] must operate each year" (Fitzgerald, 2015, p. 54).

State courts in the Land of Lincoln defer to the legislature's constitutional mandate for public education. Some observers suggest that considerations about the equity or legality of Illinois's funding program simply do not enter the court's deliberations (Fitzgerald, 2015). Judicial deference, in this instance, perpetuates inequity between high-wealth and low-wealth school districts.

Lax Accountability

The consequence that most often attends funding for privatization education is that there is no consequence. Accountability for spending public revenue is either nonexistent or lax when legislation preemptively defends funding for privatization education. For instance, "there are no provisions in the Indiana Code addressing fiscal accountability or audits" (Moon and Stewart, 2016, p. 8) for the state's voucher program.

Across the United States, "when charter schools do fail to perform as expected, they are relatively rarely held accountable under the terms of their contracts" (Baker and Miron, 2015, p. 5). As Schneider (2019) illustrates, "the grand promises of the charter movement remain unfulfilled" (para. 6). Yet, no negative sanction is often the only consequence if public funding for education is privatized and then mismanaged, inequitable, or stolen.

Consequence: Funding Misdirection

Inadequate and inequitable revenue is a feature of schooling in many states because funding is directed away from traditional public education. For instance, two-thirds of Ohio's students have become eligible for vouchers. A sizeable voucher program in South Carolina unveiled in 2019 has the potential to siphon off $500 million from public education within two years.

Observers depict a nationwide funding misdirection meant "to redefine public education as anything parents want to spend taxpayer money on" (Berkshire, 2019, para. 7).

Funding for public education is misdirected, further, by state-initiated freezes and cuts. Often imposed with little warning, the redirection or elimination of funding originally budgeted for public education has significant negative consequences. Scholars share the devastating effect of funding misdirection in New York where "freezes and cuts in state aid had a much larger impact on the districts serving the most disadvantaged students due to stronger reliance on state aid compared to wealthier districts" (Atkinson, 2019, p. 7).

Pennsylvania's school finance system was redesigned in 2008 to rectify inequities and "set a new foundation level and adopted new student-need and cost adjustments" (Baker and Corcoran, 2012, p. 18). This new student-centric approach to funding was supposed to be phased in over several years. Full implementation never occurred and the redesigned system was dismantled.

Consequence: Obstruction of the Common Good

A consequence of no small magnitude emerges from funding systems for education throughout the United States. The original constitutional intentions for free publicly funded common schools available to all have atrophied. Obstruction of the common good has become a function of public funding when privatization proponents seek free market imperatives at the public's expense.

The full scope of this 180-degree turn away from constitutional intentions for public education is represented in *Espinoza v. Montana Department of Revenue*. Plaintiffs in this case brought before the US Supreme Court sought to end the prohibitions of state constitutions against public funding of religious schools. The gist of the argument made by the plaintiffs, and the friends of the court allied with them, was "that states *must* fund religious education" (emphasis original) (Berkshire, 2019, para. 17).

In 2020, the US Supreme Court agreed with the plaintiffs "holding that if a state subsidizes private education, the Free Exercise Clause does not allow the state to deny that subsidy to a school because it is religious" (National Law Review, 2020, para. 1). In essence, the court's decision opens the door to public funding for sectarian ends when a state already provides for funding via "donations for private-school scholarship funds" (National Law Review, 2020, n.p.), otherwise known as tax credits.

Consequences of misappropriation, misdirection, or inadequate funding are in the hands of the legislators responsible for the misappropriation or inadequacy in the first place. No consequence or negative sanction is applied when public funding forswears the common good that suggests the depth of the ideology that underlies privatization funding in the first place.

Unwilling to enact "better" through education for all students using tax-payer funding, legislatures, through their own actions, become the supreme arbiter of consequences in what ought to be a system operationalized by the balance of powers.

POLICY: THE CONSEQUENCE TO RE-FUND PUBLIC EDUCATION

Policy guides the intentions that underlie public funding. Each state establishes policies on which funding decisions are made. The effect of these decisions on funding for K–12 public education are legacies that influence the lives of children, the economy of the nation, and the citizenship behaviors of adults.

No single policy priority can command 100 percent of the funding effort made by a state. But funding trade-offs illustrate how redesigning policy could alleviate the underfunding of public education:

- "U.S. states spend roughly $80 billion per year providing tax subsidies for corporations to keep or move their operations from one state to another" (Story, 2012, as cited in Suitts, 2016, p. 40). This revenue allocated annually, instead, to low-wealth districts would engage students with how to think, principled reasoning, and positive liberty.
- Spending by the states on incarceration (e.g., prison, jails) increased from 1980 to 2016 by 324 percent. During the same period, "the states' funding for public education has risen by only 107 percent" (Stullich, Morgan, & Schak, 2016, as cited in Suitts, 2016, p. 40).
- Wisconsin and Indiana's voucher programs are based on policy so malleable that voucher payments originally intended to serve low-income families tend to benefit families already enrolled in private schools. In Wisconsin, "more than 86% of the students who received vouchers in the 2016–17 school year were already attending a private school prior to receiving a voucher" (Bruecker, 2017, p. 6).

A Student-Centric Policy and Consequence for Funding

Public funding that fosters the student-centric consequences of teaching and learning is thwarted by a fixation on inputs and outputs. Inputs and outputs, it turns out, are instrumental to "better" only for a commodity.

Fixating on inputs (the resources/revenue for teaching and learning) and fixating on outputs (test scores or other trailing indicators alleged to demonstrate academic proficiency correlated with inputs) ensures division and disconnection in US education.

Division and disconnection thrive when competition for prescribed inputs and outputs drives public education and its funding. Inequity and inadequacy suffuse US education as a result of funding systems overwhelmed by these ideological imperatives.

The intentional and unintentional consequences of US education linked to funding deserve examination on behalf of all students. Shields et al. (2017) suggest that an intentional student-centric consequence of school funding develops from understanding "that what matters most is meeting a specified educational threshold" ("Equality and Adequacy," para. 1).

Baker and Corcoran (2012) argue that the quality of student learning opportunities ought to be a definition of equity buttressed by adequate funding to engage all students with dynamic instruction in all schools. There is no need for magic if funding for education is derived from student-centric criteria and outcomes. As things stand currently, however, funding priorities direct massive amounts of revenue away from public education and dictate opportunities lost and futures denied.

Chapter Eight

The Thief in the Classroom

Legislative arguments about funding levels and funding distribution and poli-cymaker attempts to maneuver funding formulas in one direction or another enable revenue for public education to rob US classrooms.

Underfunded schools steal futures; gerrymandered funding robs students of color and students in poverty. Funding formulas are the accomplices of adult-centric profit; teaching and learning are stolen. Inconsequential stan-dardized assessments abscond with both revenue and time for instruction. Meanwhile, taxpayers are hoodwinked into believing adequate funding should depend on test results and that these tests are reliable litmus tests for quality teaching and learning.

Legislators aid and abet classroom robbery further when revenue systems align with their individual areas of expertise. Life experiences in business, industry, law, or politics are lenses through which funding for dynamic teaching and learning is out of focus. Public education is misperceived as a commodity, as a market, or as the equivalent of the legislature's unruly fiscal child best disciplined through restriction, scarcity, and ideology.

These misperceptions permit funding schemes that separate students from the original power of education. Magic tricks give expression to free market theory and give leverage to authorities who adhere to the educational mecha-nisms that put this theory in motion.

Once funding systems begin to steal from students, path dependence takes hold. Inequity and inadequacy are more the norm than the exception through-out education in the United States. State authorities, in the design of school funding systems, can execute what is known colloquially as *the five-finger discount*, stealing support away from the most important, and most difficult, educational task of all: quality, dynamic instruction.

Baker et al. (2019) put this state of affairs succinctly when they find that "most states provide sufficient resources to their lowest-poverty districts and achieve above-average outcomes. The opposite is true, however, of the highest-poverty districts: they are underfunded vis-à-vis predicted requirements, and their students perform accordingly" (p. 15). Either way, few states make a funding effort commensurate with fulfilling education's most important task.

The purpose of this chapter is to discuss school funding as a thief. This chapter reflects the evidence that confirms "the fact that so many states are either non-progressive or regressive is *by design*" (emphasis original) (Baker et al., 2019, p. 19). In this case, funding system design is tantamount to classroom robbery. Designing this caper, policymakers, legislatures, and state authorities commit theft when dynamic instruction is taken from US students.

THEFT BY FUNDING: THREE EASY LESSONS

Theft by funding happens without a great deal of fanfare. At first glance, the design of funding formulas seems to recognize differences among school districts and among students:

> Almost all state school finance programs allow for some level of funding differences based on local willingness to pay for public elementary and secondary education, differences in the costs of educating various categories of high-need pupils, or differences in the costs of providing education services in different geographic areas (Skinner, 2019, p. 9).

As research makes abundantly clear, however, funding programs give only token recognition to these differences and disguise how states design funding levels and funding distribution to shortchange students, educators, schools, and learning. Theft by funding is an attribute of too many funding formulas and is carried out by policymakers who learned their craft from three easy lessons.

Lesson 1: It Wasn't Me

The first lesson learned on the way to stealing the most important task of education has two parts: denial and blame.

Denial is easy. By presuming adequate funding, policymakers deny the theft of sufficient revenue for dynamic instruction. Moreover, denial of the importance of dynamic instruction, denial of the positive impact of revenue on instruction, or denial of the competence of professional educators—cloak both the theft and the thief.

Theft is a selective behavior. Inequity and inadequacy occur predominantly in low-wealth and otherwise disenfranchised communities. Denial of these circumstances is entrenched when "bifurcated state-local funding schemes, underestimates of inflation and student need, and arbitrary school funding multipliers all serve the interests of suburbs" (Black, 2019, p. 1423).

Suburban and other high-wealth school districts have the capacity to overcome fiscal shortfalls designed into state funding systems. Scholars observe the deleterious impact of this level of theft: "the state engages in targeted partiality toward some students and denies other students the impartiality that equal protection demands" (Black, 2019, p. 1424).

Ongoing theft of dynamic instruction inspires the second part of this lesson: the blame game. Denying that funding systems have anything to do with incomplete learning, designers then shift blame to the usual suspects: educators.

Educators, a commodity, are blamed for a range of faults including ineffectiveness and falling short on a so-called "teachability index" (Scafidi, 2016, p. 130). Blame cast on educators reinforces the ideological imperative to rid the public sector of the scourge of too much government.

Blame is cast on educators by stipulating that "state statutes providing due process protections and defining tenure status for teachers are a primary cause of deficiencies in teacher qualifications, specifically in districts and schools within districts serving disadvantaged minority populations" (Black, 2016, as cited in Baker and Weber, 2016, p. 4).

When policymakers and legislators proclaim *it wasn't me* when a funding formula evinces inequity, educators are identified as the evildoers because they are unable or unwilling establish academic success using the revenue at hand.

Blame is cast, also, on students exposed to underfunded instruction. Critics of traditional public education assert that ample funding is available and that those for whom revenue is provided are the real culprits, incapable of making efficient, successful, use of it.

Denial and blame distract attention from the impact of insufficient revenue. Denial and blame steal opportunities for the dialogue required to understand how instruction is the cornerstone of school, life, and success for all students. Denial and blame ensure that purloined learning is never returned to those with the right to own it: all US students.

Lesson 2: Money Doesn't Matter

A lesson devoted to the premise that money doesn't matter, at first, makes little sense. After all, state legislatures and policymakers design sizeable budgets.

This lesson makes perfect sense, however, because it teaches to whom, and how, money doesn't matter when education finance is the budget line.

The lesson that money doesn't matter is aligned with the mantra that less government and less cost ought to be priorities of the public sector. This lesson is so ingrained that if legislated funding reforms for increased revenue yield academic improvement, the reforms are often rescinded, dismantled, or abandoned (Darling-Hammond, 2019).

Money doesn't matter is a lesson that begins with expensive preparation: more than $1.7 billion is spent on standardized tests. This expenditure establishes the premise that standardized test results are the voice and face of quality teaching and learning.

Preparation sets the stage for the lesson that emerges in findings that "the vast majority of states spend only a fraction of estimated requirements, particularly among their highest-poverty districts" (Baker et al., 2019, p. 25) to support the academic proficiency necessary for standardized testing success. The lesson comes to fruition when critics of public education expenditures point to low test scores as proof that money doesn't matter.

Funding formulas exemplify the impact of this paradoxical lesson. Sizeable funding is dedicated to standardized testing, but insufficient funding is dedicated to teaching and learning. Forcing traditional public schools to meet testing standards without access to sufficient revenue for the instruction necessary for test success is a lesson in predisposition for failure.

When teaching and learning are set up by funding insufficiencies to fail on standardized assessments, money allocated for traditional public education appears to make no difference and the low cost of privatization education is the proffered remedy.

Irony Built into the Lesson

Ironically, money does matter when for-profit EMOs, entrepreneurs, and privatization school leaders are lesson providers. For instance, a so-called *sweeps contract* is a revenue stream familiar to charter schools. This example of money *does* matter occurs when "an entrepreneur sets up a [non-profit] charter school, then hires his own company or family members to provide the critical services for the school while leasing the school building from himself" (Greene, 2019a, p. 4).

Lesson 3: Spend Not, Waste Not

Expanding mandates, burgeoning standardized testing, growing numbers of students with identified learning needs, and encroaching societal problems (e.g., drug addiction; gun violence; bullying) make their presence felt throughout US schools. At the same time, the impression takes hold that public schools are wasteful. Privatization proponents argue that bureaucracy and inefficiencies inherent in growing numbers of school personnel increase cost while they perpetuate low quality and low test results in public education (Scafidi, 2016).

Spend not, waste not, is a lesson that teaches how bureaucracy and teacher unions endow all public education with unnecessary personnel and practices that drive up the cost of education with no positive return on investment (Rogers, 2015). Legislators and state leaders from Tennessee, Florida, and New Jersey have claimed, for example, that waste in public education is endemic to the point that "'mismanagement . . . incompetence, politics, and worse' were the cause of education deficiencies in urban districts" (Black, 2019, pp. 1419–20).

To bolster ROI and ensure low cost, legislatures employ various lesson strategies, as Black (2019) enumerates:

- New York's legislature conducted an efficiency analysis that excluded information about 50 percent of the state's academically successful schools. This approach "suggests the state's primary goal was to drive down the base cost of education, not identify quality schools with efficient spending practices" (p. 1399);
- Some states use previous spending totals that underfunded schools originally, and this charade creates the baseline for estimating the cost of an adequate education in an upcoming budget cycle (p. 1399);
- Still other states "use current data but exclude inflation adjustments for upcoming budgets" (p. 1399); and
- Virginia capped the number of support personnel positions funded by the state and cut $378 million from the state's baseline revenue obligation but the cost reduction did not include a calculation of the learning lost (p. 1400).

State legislatures also act on this lesson by presupposing blame by requiring traditional public school grant recipients to share "how the funds are spent; namely, are the funds spent efficiently such that student test score performance significantly improves or are the funds spent inefficiently, increasing waste while doing little to improve student outcomes?" (Palardy et al., 2015, p. 278).

Spending on the tool (standardized testing) that sets up the impression of waste (test results), while underfunding the instruction necessary for quality teaching and learning required for test success, demonstrates the enduring lessons that inspire theft in the classroom.

Path Dependence: The Impact of Three Lessons

Rogers (2015) calls attention to the concept of *path dependence* in a narrative devoted to US education, philanthropy, and public policy. Path dependence means "that once an action is taken, it changes the relative costs of all future actions and can have large impacts over time" (p. 769). New public management, marketization, and impermanence (Ford, 2016) are actions already embedded in revenue systems of US education. These instances of path dependence point the way to an unaccountable, inequitable, and underfunded future for teaching and learning.

Path dependence is inertia. Moving away from the patterns and outcomes of school funding systems becomes more difficult over time. Lessons learned underfund public education and steal teaching and learning. The effects of funding formulas rob public education of the capacity to improve. Underfunding ossifies instructional practice. Path dependence locks short- and long-term consequences of duality within US education.

The Attributes of Path Dependence

Path dependence nurtures some vile attributes of US society. The racist intentions of private school voucher programs, for example, have never been abandoned (Fiddiman and Yin, 2019; Shaffer and Dincher, 2020; Suitts, 2019). Twenty-first century school funding formulas permit enrollment discrimination and exclusion (Fiddiman and Yin, 2019). Fiscal subterfuge (e.g., tax credit "scholarships") gives leeway to private schools and legislatures to claim no state or federal monies fund privatization. Deceit renders privatization education exempt from civil rights statutes and other legal protections.

Path dependence galvanizes discrimination to public funding for schooling that denies equity, justice, and fairness for all students. The result is nothing less than state-sponsored discrimination (Swensson et al., 2019a) derived from unrepentant path dependence. In the guise of choice and freedom, states fund teaching and learning for unprincipled, undemocratic, privatization to sustain racism and poverty.

The serious problems that infest funding for US education (e.g., inadequacy, inequity, statehouse magic tricks) foster the most consequential problem of all. Put simply, the most important task of education in the United States is stolen by misguided priorities, counterproductive lessons, and adult-centric perspectives that steal funding from dynamic instruction (Swensson and Shaffer, 2020).

EDUCATION'S MOST NEGLECTED TASK

Lessons teach policymakers and state leaders to neglect education's most important task. Dynamic instruction is in-person teaching that engages all students with the original power of education. "Dynamic instruction is the decisive means by which pedagogy validates grows, and improves the meaning-making and moral centering of all students" (Swensson and Shaffer, 2020, p. 81).

Funding for dynamic instruction is neglected, however, because it is personnel-intensive. Purchasing dynamic instruction means paying for talented educators with salaries commensurate with dynamic instruction's impact on the future. Researchers indicate that "truly compensatory resource allocation [yields] positive effects on achievement" (Weathers and Sosina, 2019, p. 7).

The neglect of revenue required to establish and sustain dynamic instruction is a bottom line disdainful of sufficient funding for education. Such neglect is a harbinger of educational disparities that fuel poverty and racism. Failure to attend to sufficient funding for dynamic instruction furthers bifurcation, dire consequences, and academic inadequacies throughout the nation's schools.

Funding for the Minimum

The academic inadequacies in US education derive, in part, from a definition of *adequate*. Educational adequacy in the United States is defined as "a legal theory that calls for the provision of a *high minimum quality* education to all of the students in a state (emphasis added)" (Umpstead, 2007, p. 285, as cited in Swensson and Shaffer, 2020, p. 51).

Since the 1990s, in an attempt to move beyond the bare minimum funding for public education often approved in court (Minorini and Sugarman, 1999), scholars have argued for funding that provided adequate opportunity for all students. This view of funding was described as a "high-minimum approach [that] focuses on what would be needed to assure that all children have access to those educational opportunities that are necessary to gain a level of learning and skills that are now required" (Minorini and Sugarman, 1999, p. 188).

DYNAMIC INSTRUCTION: WHAT THE THIEF REALLY STEALS

The presumption that some sort of minimum fulfills the responsibility of a state to invest in education is theft in its own right. Funding formulas dedicated to this presumption prevent adequate and equitable instruction sufficient to engage all US students in brighter futures. The thief in the classroom steals these futures and the dynamic instruction necessary to end path dependence on the understanding in the United States of *adequate* education as *minimum education.*

Future funding for adequacy (beyond inequitable and insufficient minimums) entails a student-centric focus on dynamic instruction and the original power of education. Dynamic instruction is a research-based investment by educators in the teaching and learning exchange in a classroom dedicated to "the intersection of *how to think* and the moral obligation of public education" (Swensson and Shaffer, 2020, p. 81).

Dynamic instruction harnesses the original power of education which "is the critical mass formed by teaching and learning as an exchange among and between intelligences" (Swensson and Shaffer, 2020, p. 68). Well-trained educators employ both *instructional precursors* and *effective evaluation* to ensure that classroom lessons challenge and extend the capabilities of all students (Swensson and Shaffer, 2020).

A host of contemporary practices exemplify the range of student-centric teaching and learning that can be fueled by future adequate and equitable funding. "Research-proven supports and interventions include high-quality preschool, extended learning time, smaller class sizes, in- and out-of-class tutoring, sufficient guidance counselors and nurses, and access to social and mental health services" (Farrie et al., 2019, p. 12).

The rationale for linking school funding with dynamic instruction is clear. For almost a century, studies have demonstrated the relationship between ample revenue and strong student achievement (Powell, 1933; Vincent, 1945). Mort and Ruesser (1951) confirmed that "expenditure level is one of the highly important factors in achieving a good education" (p. 140).

Numerous studies in the twenty-first century sustain these findings. Increased per-pupil funding dedicated to instructional reforms led to "narrowed gaps in performance on standardized tests, increased high school graduation rates, and bolstered adult success in the labor market" (Caldelaria & Shores, 2015; Card & Payne, 2002; Jackson, Johnson, & Persico, 2016; Johnson and Jackson, 2017; Lafortune, Rothstein, & Schanzenbach, 2015, as cited in Johnson and Tanner, 2018, p. 1).

Theft: Simpler than Dynamic Instruction and Its Funding

Dynamic instruction is complex and difficult. Teaching at this level requires robust funding, university-prepared professionals, and sustained investment. Theft, however, is simpler. Lowering cost, underfunding, or funding formula manipulation ease the way for policymakers and ideologues dedicated to "better" as a function of the minimums of ideology and not learning.

The theft of revenue necessary for dynamic instruction throughout US schools is accomplished with relative ease and with surprising state-to-state similarities. For instance, between 2009–2010 and 2016–2017, a total of forty-two states "decreased their average annual salary for public school teachers" (Rentner, 2019, p. 4). Path dependence takes hold and affects funding and the quality of instruction. "There are still 170,000 fewer jobs in public education than there were before the recession, despite public school enrollment being 1.5 million higher" (American Federation of Teachers [AFT], 2018).

Undercut by performance measures and manipulated funding, the most important task in education—creating and delivering dynamic instruction to engage all students with how to think—is stolen from traditional public schools and their students.

IN THE FUNDING DEGRADATION ZONE

Public education is a daunting responsibility. Revenue is necessary to fulfill the responsibility of legislatures for public education. Funding formulas, thus, reveal intents and priorities. Students and their futures, societies and their prospects, governments and their principles, economies and their functions all are on display in the funding and the responsibilities a society provides as answers to the test of public education.

Baker (2014) sketches the impact of this display on US schooling. "There have been clear and large funding disparities in education. These occur when general state aid formulas fail by simply providing too little state aid to improve equity" (Baker, 2014, p. 5). Revenue disappears and the constitutional responsibility of each state for teaching and learning goes with it.

Educational gerrymandering (Black, 2019) fragments education. Bifurcation separates and disconnects education. Education becomes synonymous with *the minimum.* These factors are indigenous to destination, the funding degradation zone (FDZ), from which revenue for traditional public education never returns.

In the Zone: The Scofflaw Capacity

The first element in the FDZ that ensures the disappearance of revenue is the *scofflaw capacity.* Although regulations, rules, and statutes establish boundaries for the conduct and accountability of the public sector, there is a capacity—often built-in to legislation and practice—that scoffs at regulation of education and its funding. The scofflaw capacity is a powerful factor in the zone and is represented in several examples:

- "Charter school legislation often has been poorly crafted and nonspecific as to the actual application of the overall education finance distribution formula" (Wood, 2019, "Public or Private Actors," para. 1).
- Georgia's tax credit scholarship program, on paper, is in place to give all parents and caregivers choice for education. But some private schools—while the legislature and courts look the other way—guarantee scholarship support to the children or other designees of parents and caregivers who donate to the tax credit scholarship program that is associated with a specific private school.

   Essentially, contributions to a tax credit scholarship program become tuition payments "despite the fact that donors are technically prohibited under the law from designating their own dependents as beneficiaries" (Levin, 2013, p. 1063).
- The bifurcation of education into separate perspectives puts states in position to create funding formulas that incorporate less than adequate tax rates. School districts are left to pick up the shortfall (Black, 2019).
- Between 2000 and 2017, state funding for charter schools in Texas increased by 640 percent from a total expenditure of $300 million to $2.2 billion (Villanueva, 2019, p. 2).
- Twelve separate funding formulas developed by Pennsylvania's legislature in 2013 supposedly addressed underfunding across the state's five hundred school districts. Instead, "these twelve formulas sent funds to just twenty-one [districts]" (Black, 2019, p. 1411).
- Mississippi's funding formula disappears because the legislature "refuses to allocate the funds that the formula indicates schools need. Mississippi has only fully funded its formula four times in twenty years" (Black, 2019, pp. 1411–12).
- In 2011, New Jersey reduced its budget for education by $1.6 billion. "'The districts with high concentrations of at-risk children . . . lost $687 million or $1530 per pupil,' whereas wealthy districts lost only $944 per pupil" (Black, 2019, p. 1417).
- "In 2015, North Carolina exerted the third least school funding effort in the nation. From 2013–2015, North Carolina doubled its charter school funding and instituted enormous tax cuts for the wealthiest individuals in the state" (Black, 2019, p. 1418).

The scofflaw capacity entails legislative resistance, inaction, or design and "operates under the premise that the legislature has the authority to decide for itself whether it has met its constitutional duty" (Black, 2019, p. 1429). This premise contravenes the basic legal principle asserted by both the US Supreme Court and state supreme courts that the duty of the judiciary is to interpret what the law is and that legislatures cannot employ legislative action to disagree with judicial rulings (Black, 2019).

In the Zone: A Blind Eye to History

The second factor associated with the disappearance of funding in the FDZ is what will be referred to as a *blind eye to history.* If the nineteenth and twentieth centuries provide any insight into aspects of US education it would be an insight into discrimination, underfunding, and inequity.

Unfortunately, policymakers, lawmakers, and educators closed their eyes to these flaws. Rolling into the twenty-first century, the blind eye to history shows up in findings that:

> districts reporting higher levels of funding are more likely to be located in communities where student poverty is minimal, whereas those reporting lower levels of funding are more often located in communities where student poverty is sizable (National Center for Education Statistics, 2000b, as cited in Biddle and Berliner, 2002, p. 51).

US history is replete with White privilege; emerging in education in the form of *stereotype threat, marginalization,* and *deficit thinking* (Swensson et al., 2019b). Tragically and unnecessarily disconnected from social justice, fairness, and principled reasoning, these impediments to learning and living for students of color extend the despicable minimums of funding for US schools.

Ladd et al. (2018), highlight the blind eye to history represented in "the increasing racial imbalance across charter schools in the state" of North Carolina (p. 1). "Evidence from ethnic fragmentation literature suggests that people are less willing to fund public spending when there is a perception that the public goods will be shared with out-group members" (Alesina, Baqir, and Easterly 1999, as cited in Weaver and Sosina, 2019, p. 13).

The history of school funding in the United States bears out these examples of racism. Local taxation to support public education has been manipulated on behalf of segregation. "Some states, for instance, kept white taxes for white schools and black taxes for black schools. Some also gave white communities the power to issue bonds to support their schools while denying that power to blacks" (Black, 2019, p. 1421).

Turning a blind eye to history is turning a blind eye to history's failures and to education's neglect of its moral obligation (Swensson and Shaffer, 2020).

Virtual, online, and so-called "hybrid learning" exemplify the FDZ's capacity for swallowing quality education. Contemporary teaching often called *distance learning* or *virtual education* replicates the abject failure of a less technological mirror image from history known as the Lancasterian Method.

Simply put, the Lancasterian Method was the brainchild of a British educator in the nineteenth century designed to maximize efficiency and reduce cost. The basic idea of this method was that older students would "instruct" younger students under the supervision of a limited number of adults. Class sizes approached one hundred students. The small number of adult teachers greatly reduced cost.

Distance learning in the twenty-first century resurrects large numbers of students "learning" via infrequent technological interaction with adults. Terribly worrisome is student access to a myriad of illicit, hate-filled, or dangerous Internet sources in the absence of ongoing adult interaction within a classroom. Equally alarming is the absence online of dynamic instruction, the moral obligation of public education, and the original power of education.

This section of the FDZ encapsulates the discriminatory potential in limiting the role of the public sector to self-aggrandizing economic singularity; sizeable profit is a feature of virtual schooling.

In the Zone: Public Funds for Sectarian Ends

The third factor in the FDZ is *public funds for sectarian ends.* Public funding for vouchers can pay for students to attend religious schools. This means, among other things, that public revenue pays for the teaching of creationism, for daily readings of scripture, or a curriculum based on the principles of a religious belief. Paid for with tax funding, these practices "infringe upon basic principles of religious liberty by providing public funds for sectarian proselytizing" (Weaver, 2018, para. 13).

Indiana's voucher program is an early and textbook example of public funding for religious private education. Advertised as a program for low-income families stuck in poorly performing public schools, Indiana's vouchers quickly morphed into a pattern of payments to students with "prior private school attendance and a significant portion of participants who are not low-income" (Bruecker, 2017, p. 6).

In 2018–2019, $161 million from taxpayers in Indiana paid for vouchers and 99.4 percent of that total went to religious schools (Miksza, Robinson, and Schlegel-Ruegger, 2019).

When the US Supreme Court in 2020 ruled in favor of the plaintiffs in *Rodriguez v. Montana Board of Revenue*, significant latitude was given to state funding for sectarian ends. The likelihood that many more states will enable public funding for religious private education to follow Montana and Indiana increases the potential for disappearing revenue in this section of the zone.

The Zone and the Commodity

Disappearing revenue has a significant impact on who teaches and how teaching occurs. The effects of the FDZ ensure a commodity that delivers on-the-cheap instruction:

- "Using data from the National Center for Education statistics, we find that tax limits systematically reduce the average quality of education majors, as well as new public school teachers in states that have passed these limits" (Baker and Weber, 2016, p. 10).
- "A substantial body of literature has accumulated to validate the conclusions that teachers' overall wages and relative wages affect the quality of those who choose to enter the teaching profession—and whether they stay once they get in" (Baker et al., 2016, p. 4).
- Studies find that teachers in districts with higher salaries relative to non-teaching salaries in the same county are less likely to leave teaching and that a teacher is less likely to change districts when he or she teachers in a district near the top of the teacher salary distribution in that county (Baker and Weber, 2016, p. 10).
- Research "found that 'increases in teacher salaries are associated with noticeable decreases in the proportions of teachers who are newly hired, uncredentialed, or less well educated'" (Baker and Weber, 2016, p. 10).

STOLEN BUT NOT FORGOTTEN

Funding formulas are thieves. Well-trained educators, engaged learning, robust and varied curriculum all are stolen when funding neglects the most important task of US public education. Inadequate and inequitable state funding formulas perpetuate teaching and learning that robs all students of capabilities required for life success in the twenty-first century.

Theft by funding exists, in part, because legislative inaction and path dependence sell educators and students short. Denial and blame are among the lessons that policymakers learn to ensure preservation of the funding status quo.

Underfunding breeds employment instability for public educators and learning inadequacy for public school students. Revenue that otherwise would raise salaries and decrease teacher-to-student ratios disappears.

Few states reform funding formulas despite ample evidence that increased revenue restores what disappears too often from public schools and the students served there. Unacknowledged and unresolved, theft by funding means that students experience teaching and learning that is a function of the vagaries of location, economics, race, legislative sleight of hand, and ideological tomfoolery.

Theft by funding is a sustained, damaging, and divisive characteristic of US education. Funding formula manipulation, free market theory, and intentional disparities undermine student-centric teaching and learning. Dualities exacerbate the deleterious impact of funding and envelop public education in a hazy understanding of role and purpose. Under these circumstances, the thief in the classroom exacts a terrible cost on the lives and futures of students.

If the future of public education is to foster the common good while engaging all students in learning that is fulfilling and challenging, then a bottom line for revenue in education must be considered.

The present-day inability of funding and those responsible for funding to direct revenue to a bottom line reflective of the common good in US society drains public education of its potential and subverts its promises. Identifying this bottom line, despite the titanic forces and factors that provide inadequacy and inequity throughout funding for public education, is the first step in restoring a role for education that incorporates its most important task.

Chapter Nine

Funding for Public Education

Is There a Bottom Line?

The grab bag of problems and prizes for funding public education holds a clue to the enduring failure of revenue systems to establish adequate and equitable schooling. Influenced by ideological perspectives, subject to manipulation, and fragmented, funding for US public education develops from a severely limited interpretation of *the bottom line*.

One interpretation of the bottom line dominates funding formulas and the impact of funding systems on teaching and learning. This one interpretation limits the bottom line of school funding to the *measurement of total cost*. This view equates the value of teaching and learning with an accounting of their *purchase price*. Interpreting funding formulas and the public schools they pay for relies exclusively on bottom line calculations as if only numbers indicate either the worth, or the waste, fostered by public education.

This interpretation, though, is incomplete. There are two additional interpretations essential to determining a bottom line for US public education. The first depicts the bottom line as *criterion*. This interpretation of the bottom line constitutes the principle (e.g., equity, *how to think*, dynamic instruction, adequacy) chosen to guide the use or application of revenue for instruction and educational programs. This interpretation provides a baseline from which school districts judge congruence among decisions, strategies, and actions and the adopted criterion. The second depicts the bottom line as *outcome*. This interpretation of the bottom line constitutes the way instruction and instructional programs turn out in positive learning impact for all students. This interpretation allows school districts to monitor and adjust instruction and programming to improve the way learning engages with and is expressed by all students.

The purpose of this chapter is to discuss how the incomplete view of the bottom line for school funding erects numerous barriers to the meaning and success of US public education. Presupposing that the bottom line for educational funding is only measurement of total cost initiates innumerable inadequacies and disparities throughout public education. Buried under an avalanche of numbers, *criterion* and *outcome* do not guide policymakers' determination of the bottom line for funding public education.

The enduring dilemma created by the incomplete bottom line is that nine out of every ten students in the United States are robbed, underserved in classrooms where funding fails to deliver dynamic teaching and learning. This chapter examines how the incomplete interpretation of the bottom line for funding US public education aids and abets the thief in the classroom.

AN INCOMPLETE BOTTOM LINE: THE ABSENCE OF *CRITERION* AND *OUTCOME*

The incomplete interpretation of the bottom line for funding either facilitates or undermines the two major perspectives about US education. On the one hand, measurement of total cost is the only description of the bottom line required for privatization education. On the other hand, measurement of total cost, alone, undermines the bottom line of traditional public education.

Measurement of total cost facilitates less (e.g., cost, government) and aligns with the intentions of privatization education. By comparison, the incomplete interpretation of the bottom line, the absence of *criterion* and *outcome*, undermines the intentions of traditional public education. The consequences that arise from measurement of total cost fulfill one perspective about US education and prevent investment by the other.

The role of the public sector is foretold by each of these interpretations of the bottom line for school funding. When the bottom line for school funding is only measurement of total cost, the role of the public sector is incomplete, fulfilled by privatization education and the reduction of cost. When interpretation of the bottom line for school funding systems interconnects criterion and outcome, the role of the public sector is investment in traditional public education.

WHEN THE BOTTOM LINE ISN'T

The bottom line for US education is its own conundrum. Reliance on measurement of total cost to interpret the bottom line of school funding is the escape route that policymakers and state authorities take when, inevitably, funding formulas fail the test of education.

This incomplete interpretation of the bottom line abandons students, dynamic instruction, and the original power of education. Supplanting criterion and outcome with measurement of total cost ensures that the incomplete interpretation of the bottom line for school funding is the road to inequity and inadequacy.

Path dependence glues lawmakers to this incomplete interpretation of the bottom line. Disparities engendered by measurement of total cost are sustained and render teaching and learning inert. Funding divorced from criterion and outcome facilitates incomplete instructional programs that dictate stagnant futures for individuals, US democracy, and the nation's economy. These futures, in turn, perpetuate the cycle of underfunding, desiccated instruction, counterproductive testing, and anemic academic results that lead to more misdirected, disparity-laden, funding.

The incomplete interpretation of the bottom line prohibits attention to criterion and outcome used to forge revenue focused on student-centric instruction. Teaching and learning that bring "better" and the common good to the fore in all US classrooms, thus, are underfunded. Inequity, academic insufficiency, and multiple disparities are characteristics of US education fostered by the limitations inherent in the incomplete interpretation of the bottom line of school funding.

At the Bottom Line: Equity for Whom?

Privatization education, promoted from the 1990s into the twenty-first century, is touted by proponents "as cutting edge and a significant catalyst for redefining the traditional landscape of the American public school system" (Gallo, 2014, pp. 209–10).

As such, this perspective and the incomplete interpretation of the bottom line that it supports imply a positive education for all US students. But, as one observer of charter schools in Pennsylvania indicated, critics "argued that the charter school concept 'was less about helping kids stuck in bad schools than it was about furthering an anti-government agenda'" (Gallo, 2014, p. 212).

Equity, as too many funding formulas demonstrate, is a factor missing from contemporary interpretation of the bottom line of school funding. Incomplete interpretation of the bottom line of funding invokes no criterion except *less* to guide funding level and distribution of revenue. Building on a criterion, like equity, establishes a purpose for funding beyond merely measuring numbers and ensuring lower cost.

The incomplete interpretation of the bottom line and the ideological pursuit of less, surprisingly does attend to equity. Instead of equity for students, equity for taxpayers is often the baseline for school funding (Knoeppel et al.,

2013). Equity for students is, at best, a lower priority embedded in the bottom line interpretations and revenue choices of legislatures. Equity for students, at worst, is state discrimination that privileges one cohort of students over others.

Inequity is no stranger in funding formulas anchored by the incomplete interpretation of the bottom line for school funding when, by design, different localities are revenue-preferenced. "The state's decision regarding the percentage of education costs it will cover is ultimately a decision about how much it will spare the suburbs or meet the needs of districts serving high percentages of at-risk students" (Black, 2019, p. 1409).

Prioritizing the bottom line for school funding in this way activates future-risk: Underfunded and underserved by traditional public education, ineffective instructional programs are foisted on millions of students by insufficient revenue. This means the future for the economy, the arts, innovations, and societal improvement is not "better," but it is less.

Funding Equity for No One

Equitable funding is an oxymoron throughout US education. Research findings demonstrate the absence of vertical equity in state funding for traditional public education (Knoeppel et al., 2013).

On the flip side of the perspectives about education, proponents complain vociferously about insufficient funding for privatization education (DeAngelis, Wolf, Maloney, and May, 2018). Meanwhile, taxpayers bemoan the high cost of taxation for public education and passage of referendums or claiming victory in school tax elections becomes more difficult (Lifto and Nicol, 2019).

With equity for no one, funding for teaching and learning in the United States yields inadequate, often discriminatory, revenue for traditional public education. Inadequacies afflict low-wealth localities and their schools, while funding formulas or statutes permit high-wealth communities to augment local funding that, in and of itself, exacerbates inequity.

These circumstances illuminate the enduring, difficult, and often damaging struggle between interpretations of the bottom line for school funding often portrayed as an either-or forced choice: efficiency or effectiveness.

Baseline Bifurcation, Baseline Inequity

Bifurcation—two fundamentally different perspectives about public education—conflated with an incomplete interpretation of the bottom line for funding education, establishes inequitable school funding as a baseline. Stretching state budgets to fund traditional education while privatization education grows "imposes clear fiscal pressures on local school districts in the short run" (Ladd and Singleton, 2018, "Charter School Growth," para. 2).

Moreover, inequity multiplies when students move to choice education from traditional schooling. The loss of per-pupil revenue when this occurs in a school district already underfunded by a state can have a devastating impact on teaching and learning quality. Inequity is multiplied when underfunded public schools located in a community are unable to accommodate the lost revenue by increasing local taxation (Ladd and Singleton, 2018).

Inequity Is a Future

The prevalence of inequitable funding alongside achievement disparities speaks to the disastrous effects of educational gerrymandering. Legislatures across the United States create ineffective funding systems that leave low-wealth communities and students of color without access to schools that deliver the full measure of "better."

Educational gerrymandering sustains inequity. Put bluntly, "the segregation of resources, with greater resources flowing to children from families in the upper quintiles of society, makes it highly unlikely that children from the lower quintiles can have an equal chance of achieving success" (Shields, Newman, and Satz, 2017). Democracy's bulwark, traditional public education, supports inequity for the future when criterion and outcome disappear in the presence of measurement of total cost. The incomplete interpretation of the bottom line of school funding is the ultimate segregation of resources.

At the Bottom Line: Insufficient Achievement

When measurement of total cost is the sole determinant of the bottom line, criterion and outcome are suspended. The incomplete interpretation of the bottom line launches insufficient student achievement.

In the absence of criterion and outcome to interpret the bottom line for funding, student academic proficiency (e.g., how to think, principled reasoning, positive liberty) is dormant. Dynamic instruction is forsaken for test prep. Student achievement disintegrates under these conditions.

The capabilities of all students for robust achievement are nurtured only where underfunding and disparity are arrested by local high wealth. The incomplete view of the bottom line for school funding engenders hapless levels of student achievement:

- Research about Indiana's voucher program "found that students who used vouchers did not see academic gains in their new schools and that they performed worse, on average, than their matched peers in the public schools they left" (Boser et al., 2018, "An Overview," para. 3).

- An evaluation of Louisiana's voucher program revealed "declines that are the equivalent of the average math student—at the 50th percentile— dropping to the 34th percentile after three years of participation in the Louisiana voucher program" (Bose et al., 2018, "An Overview," para. 6).
- In Ohio, research indicates that negative academic performance in both math and reading is associated with voucher school attendance (Boser et al., 2018).
- An evaluation of private schooling in 2010 found that "on average, private schools offer 65.5 minutes less per week in reading instruction and 48.3 minutes less per week in math instruction" (Boser et al., 2018, "Explaining the Negative," para. 3).
- Charter school advocates contend that standardized test scores lower than or equal to traditional public school scores are irrelevant because charter schools are "endowing students with skills, knowledge, work habits, motivation, and values that are important for long-term success but are not fully captured by test scores" (Sass et al., 2016, p. 685).

At the Bottom Line: Artful Revenue Recalcitrance

State legislatures create funding formulas and related statutes to enact a version of public education sketched by language in the state's constitution. The incomplete interpretation of the bottom line for funding education guides an incomplete education. Funding formulas established from this bottom line evince the practice of *artful revenue recalcitrance*.

Legislative recalcitrance occurs when the design of revenue for education thwarts principles of justice. Ignoring state and federal laws that confirm and protect civil rights, legislatures condone funding formulas for mechanisms that ensure the denial of basic rights for students. A study of the sixty-two different voucher programs in the United States:

found that only 11 of them, or 18 percent, included state specific language against sex-based discrimination. Additionally, just seven programs, or 11 percent, enumerated state-specific protections against discrimination on the basis of sexual orientation, and only three programs, or 5 percent, included protections for gender identity (Fiddiman and Yin, 2019, "Sex-based Discrimination," para. 3).

Unwilling to ensure the protection of the rights of all students whose education is funded, directly or indirectly by state funding schemes, legislative recalcitrance also fosters profiteering. The role of the public sector as a common good is turned upside down when state funding is given over to profiteering.

Scholars depict this phenomenon in Pennsylvania where "charter school profiteers have become proverbial parasites siphoning public funds meant for the education of Pennsylvania's youth, morphing the charter school movement into the 'financialization of public education'" (Gallo, 2014, p. 215).

At the Bottom Line: Fragmentation Is Successful Failure

Successful failure is an oxymoron. But this term describes accurately the effect of the multiple dualities that infest public education and its funding. Funding fragmentation is accepted by state authorities and policymakers because fragmented revenue systems for education offer two advantages.

First, funding two opposing perspectives about education gives "cover" to those responsible for allocating state funds if complaints about insufficient revenue arise. Because one of the perspectives expresses the bottom line for school funding as the calculation of less cost, complaints about inadequate funding can be sidelined by claims of inefficiency and waste as the "cause" of funding shortfalls.

Second, fragmented funding justifies underfunding and unfunded mandates. Cloaked in the excuse that state budgets are stretched to the breaking point by dual funding streams for schools, proponents of low-cost teaching and learning turn to the mantra of do-more-with-less to ward off the realities of insufficient student learning undercut by inadequate revenue for instructional programming.

Fragmented funding for US education distracts attention from the impact of funding dedicated to dynamic instruction and instructional programs. Research indicates that unfragmented funding directed at the most important task of education yields significant academic success for students (Jackson et al., 2016).

Increased funding for instruction in public education has a history of facilitating successful and important learning outcomes for all US students. Between 1980 and 2012, for example, the US GAO reported that NAEP scores in mathematics and reading increased for all public school student cohorts in age groups 9, 13, and 17. The GAO report indicated that during this same period the NAEP "scores of Black and Hispanic students improved more than those of White students" (GAO, 2018).

A study of funding in Michigan found that "a 60% increase in spending increases the percent satisfactory score by one standard deviation" (Baker, 2016, p. 7). Improved test scores are linked in the research to increases in teacher salaries and reductions in class size.

COMPETITION: WINNING OR LOSING IS THE BOTTOM LINE

The fragmentation of US education facilitates survival of the fittest invoked by the incomplete bottom line for school funding. Bifurcation fuels vilification, an *us versus them* struggle, that enshrines competition between "winners" and "losers" throughout US education. "Winning" is alleged to be independent, unregulated, low-cost teaching and learning galvanized to the incomplete bottom line for educational finance without any evidence that these "victories" are accurate or truly student-centric (Gallo, 2014).

Free market theory places a great deal of faith in the benefits of competition. One of these benefits is that winning for one school is losing for another. Free market adherents applaud the persistent closing of choice schools enabled by competition. But this nonsensical and chaotic version of musical chairs for schools has a deleterious impact on teaching and learning and heightens the unpredictability and imprecision of funding for public education.

As privatization schools come and go, winners—the choice schools with strong enrollment—are supposed to inspire improvement in traditional public schools because the innovations that allegedly litter the practices of privatization winners create robust standardized test scores. Traditional public education is expected to respond to and mimic the instructional excellence of privatization education winners as the means to replicate the supposedly strong achievement despite the fact that few studies document either instructional innovation or robust achievement emerging from privatization.

Winners, of course, can become losers. Because only a paltry research base indicates that privatization schools foster higher test scores on average than do traditional public schools (Baker and Miron, 2015), and because privatization schools tend to close because of mismanagement or fiscal malfeasance (Gilblom and Sang, 2019), competition appears to have little if anything to do with academic improvement or proficiency.

In privatization education, the research base that identifies why choice schools close is ignored. In place of research, the collapse of enrollment numbers is used by choice education proponents to identify loser schools.

Exacerbating the effects of the incomplete interpretation of the bottom line, competition promoted by privatization education advocates fails to account for the finite number of school-age students in any locality. Seeking to implement a successful business model based on measurement of total cost alone, free market schooling entrepreneurs can flood a locality with start-up schools. Under these conditions and in this marketplace, "the inevitable result is an increased number of schools for the same population of students" (Lafer, 2018, p. 13). This emphasizes back-to-business winning and losing to the detriment of students and their learning.

The rush to be a "winner" in terms suitable to an incomplete interpretation of the bottom line of school finance induces competition without regard for its dizzying impact on learning, equity, or school stability. Students become losers; competition among schools is an adult version of musical chairs carried out to realize a bottom line that sells "better" short.

Many Ways to Be a "Loser"

When it comes to traditional public schools, enrollment is not an effective measure of competition because all students are welcome. So public schools are designated as losers based on standardized test results. These schools with loser test scores can be designated to receive school improvement grants (SIGs).

In the decade between 2008 and 2018, SIGs were "the largest federal investment to date—to improve performance in struggling schools" (Kahlenberg, 2017, as cited in Waddington and Berends, 2018, p. 783).

When "loser" schools receive a SIG, several choices are offered as the means necessary to start "winning." Among the choices: restarting the school as a charter school, bringing in a new principal, firing the majority of the staff, or closing the school entirely and transferring students to a higher-performing school elsewhere in the same school district.

"Winners" on an Uneven Playing Field

Competition in the realm of public education proves to be an ideological imperative instead of a viable strategy or policy that entails improved teaching and learning. For example, the total SIG investment of $7 billion from the federal government "did not have a significant impact on improving student outcomes" (Waddington and Berends, 2018, p. 783).

In addition, competition fostered by educational gerrymandering leads to the funding capacity of each locality pitted against the capacity of all other communities in a state. Ideology "wins" in New Jersey when "payments to charter schools have first priority in district spending—they cannot be reduced to address shortfalls in the district budget" (Farrie, 2018, p. 6). An intentionally uneven playing field advantages "winners" during the school funding game but only a few of the victors are students.

Referees for Funding: Calling the Game before It Starts

Magic and consequences for winners and losers in the school funding game are exercised by referees prior to the start of competition. State legislators are the referees in this contest and call the game before it starts using their preconceived notions about the bottom line. These notions, expressed in formulas, programs, grants, statutes, and systems about school funding, are illustrated by several representative "calls" that predetermine the results of the school funding game:

- "Inarticulate statutory guidance, or statutory vagueness, that permeates charter school legislation . . . was developed by largely reiterating what another legislature had previously created" (Wood, 2019, "Conclusions," para. 2). Cookie-cutter legislation perpetuates not only a laissez-faire approach to funding privatization education but also sustains abandonment of funding oversight on behalf of all students.
- "Higher property wealth translates into higher revenues and the relationship is largely driven by 'voluntary' contributions from local school districts" (Combs et al., 2018, p. 247).
- Funding formulas manipulate and gerrymander revenue. Moreover, in both privatization education and traditional public education, private dollars exacerbate funding disparities. Elite public schools in high-wealth neighborhoods, for example, often benefit by creating "nonprofit organizations to funnel private aid to augment public support" (Kitzmiller, 2019, pp. 14–15).
- Standardized tests are a false bottom line for funding quality in teaching and learning because (i) the results of these exams have no relationship with improved student cognition; (ii) the tests reduce instruction to test prep; and (iii) the price of testing public school students throughout the nation steal revenue that could be used to hire teachers, reduce class size, and establish meaningful student-to-teacher ratios.

DECISION-MAKING: BOTTOM LINE OR "BETTER"?

Allegiance to an incomplete interpretation of the bottom line for school funding is a choice that rivets funding formulas to dualities. This choice enables fragmentation which, in turn, facilitates inadequate instruction as one of a myriad educational disparities throughout US education. Present-day bifurcation throughout US public education traps the future for teaching and learning between an incomplete bottom line and "better."

The incomplete interpretation of educational finance is evidence of the effect of path dependence. Restricted to the interpretation of education represented only by measurement of total cost, teaching and learning in the United States are handcuffed to a future of inequity and missed opportunity. "Better" is not a choice for funding public education when path dependence mandates measurement of total cost as the bottom line.

If "better" is to develop as the choice made by policymakers for funding systems throughout the United States, a fundamentally different framework for funding formulas must emerge. Within this framework must be funding systems understood as evolving hybrids composed of an underlying criterion, an ultimate outcome, and a fiscal accounting.

"Better" embodies complex interaction between criterion and outcome fashioned in response to the question *what is education*. To purchase this interaction, an interpretation of the bottom line for revenue must also evolve.

Interpreting funding systems as an evolving hybrid, in support of dynamic instruction, necessitates decision-making about the steps required to alleviate, then eliminate, the negative effects of fragmentation. These decisions represent the expansion of purpose and intent necessary if student-centric funding is to replace the incomplete bottom line of funding and its counterproductive effect on teaching and learning.

These decisions, further, represent the extent of the reform of the interpretation of the bottom line that lies ahead if legislators and policymakers are to forswear path dependence as the bedrock of educational finance:

- Private entities and privately governed entities are not required to guarantee constitutional rights to employees or to students (Baker and Miron, 2015). *The Decision*—Should all entities that receive funding directly or indirectly from state-originated or statutorily permitted sources (e.g., tuition tax credits) be required to uphold all constitutionally guaranteed rights?
- Insufficient funding for dynamic instruction and inadequate funding for low-wealth school districts plague teaching and learning throughout the United States. *The Decision*—Should states declare a moratorium on funding privatization education until insufficiency, inadequacy, and inequity are eliminated for all traditional public school districts?
- Opaque management practices and less than transparent budgetary decisions are permitted by statutes, regulations, and rules that foster absent or lax oversight for privatization schools that receive direct or indirect taxpayer-generated funding. *The Decision*—Should all statutes, regulations, and rules ensure clear and transparent accounting for all taxpayer-generated funding supplied to privatization schools?
- Standardized testing is an expensive and ineffective assessment system designed primarily to tie teaching and learning to test prep and to stimulate low-cost schools despite the prevalence of low test scores associated with inadequately funded instruction. *The Decision*—Should standardized

testing be eliminated and a fiscal emphasis on dynamic instruction be promulgated to establish "better" as the instructional baseline for funding US
education?

- Limited resources are cited time and again as the culprit that steals robust
  student achievement. Further, test scores abscond with the public's percep-
  tions of quality and institutional legitimacy of schools and school districts
  despite the irrelevance of testing to higher-order cognition, creativity, and
  problem-solving. *The Decision*—Should the Catch-22 arising from low
  test scores sustained by inadequate resources that lead to less taxpayer support for increased resources for public schools be ended with the elimination of standardized testing by statute in all states?
- Neither of the two major educational perspectives is funded sufficiently.
  Moreover, because the two are in competition and because competition
  entails the sudden closure of any privatization school, traditional public
  schools must have "sufficient excess capacity to assure that all children
  will be served should charters shut down" (Ladd and Singleton, 2018,
  "Reducing Fiscal Burdens," para. 2). *The Decision*—Should states end
  the bifurcation of school funding to both major perspectives to ensure an
  evolving hybrid provides dynamic instruction for all students across all
  traditional public schools without the foreclosure of learning related to
  competition?

Escape from an Incomplete Bottom Line: "Better"

Deciding to interpret school funding as an evolving hybrid means returning
to the regularly abandoned intentions of state constitutions. As the Kansas
Supreme Court explained, "'[M]atters intended for permanence are placed in
constitutions for a reason—to protect them from the vagaries of politics or
majority'" (Black, 2019, p. 1431).

As an evolving hybrid, funding formulas encompass criterion and outcome
as the guides from which the sufficiency of total funding for teaching and
learning can be calculated. "Better" can be crafted on behalf of students when
funding systems escape from an inadequate and incomplete interpretation of
the bottom line.

To seek "better," funding formulas with criterion and outcome at the core
of interpretation invest, first, in well-trained and well-compensated personnel. School staff, in all roles, bolster teaching and learning. The positive influence of teachers on the learning and lives of students depends on adequate
funding that supports dynamic learning opportunities for all students.

Adequacy, given this interpretation, is provided by *real resource equity*,
which requires "that per pupil spending not be perfectly equal if, for ex-

ample, resources such as similarly qualified teachers come at a higher price (competitive wage) in one region than another. *Real resource* parity is more meaningful than mere dollar equity" (Baker et al., 2016, p 5).

The reform of the interpretation of school funding, an evolving hybrid in which criterion and outcome guide sufficient revenue for instruction and instructional programs, is "better" that only rarely emerges from contemporary funding formulas. For example, as Weaver and Sosina (2019) point out, "achievement outcomes for low-income students were highest in states that invested more in education" (p. 6). Increased spending fostered by SFRs—that target quality teaching and dynamic instruction—yield student-centered procedures and results (Darling-Hammond, 2019).

"For low-income children, a 10% increase in per pupil spending each year for all 12 years of public school is associated with 0.46 additional years of completed education, 9.6% higher earnings, and a 6.1 percentage point reduction in the annual incidence of adult poverty" (Jackson et al., 2016, p. 160).

The limited interpretation placed by states on funding level, taxes, and expenditures, however, obstruct development of an evolving hybrid and the relationship between greater investment and higher achievement. "States implement policies that affect local taxes, education spending, and decisions regarding school district funding" (Weaver and Sosina, 2019, p. 9).

Funding chaos and funding manipulation ensure that funding formulas provide incomplete and ineffective resources for education. Laden with disparities enforced by measurement of total cost, US education and "better" are disconnected from funding robust learning for all students.

Policy Implications for "Better"

With present-day US education disconnected from "better" in too many localities, the future becomes the ground on which the school funding "better" must be constructed. Looking to the future, the capacity of US public education to support democracy, invest in the fulfillment of the promises of US citizenship, and engage all students with successful life choices depends on decisions about state policies that support these goals. Among the policy implications of establishing a funding interpretation for "better" in US public education are:

- "In general, teacher wages must be sufficiently competitive with other career opportunities for similarly educated individuals" (Baker et al., 2016, p. 6).
- Confusion and contention over whether public education is a fundamental right established by the constitution of each state puts the future of teaching and learning provided by public funding in limbo.

   Policy to eliminate this tentative state of affairs requires attention to the
wording of a state's constitution and, where necessary, a commitment to
amending the document (Rowe, 2010). Fundamental rights are the guaran-
tors of democracy and education as a fundamental right is the lifeblood of
citizenship and a vibrant future economy.
- "The estimated benefits to increased school spending are large enough to
  justify the increased spending under most reasonable benefit-cost calculations" (Jackson et al., 2016, p. 213).

WHEN THE BOTTOM LINE IS LESS

The incomplete interpretation of the bottom line of school funding supports
less throughout US schools. Both traditional public education and privatization education are assailed by less. Findings from a study of Indiana's
voucher program, for example, raise "questions about the mechanisms that
may explain these negative effects [for voucher-involved students] in mathematics, such as the mathematics curriculum, instruction, or teacher quality
in private schools not being as robust as is found in public schools" (Waddington and Berends, 2018, p. 803).

   Less is the result of school funding for traditional public education. The
funding lost by public schools in Oakland and San Diego referenced earlier
in this narrative meant that (i) Oakland could not reduce class size to 18 students in all elementary schools while doubling the number of counselors and
nurses throughout the school system; and (ii) San Diego could not "realize
its long-standing goal of creating 15-student classes for grades K–2, and hire
more teachers' aides" (Lafer, 2018, p. 6).

   The struggle to assert "better" despite the incomplete interpretation of
the bottom line of funding for public education also finds expression in the
enduring tension between the public good and individual goods. On the one
hand, education and its funding are privatized by a bottom line where people
are allowed "to educate children in schools that inculcate their values" (Barnum, 2019).

   The incomplete interpretation of the bottom line thwarts the common good
of an educated citizenry. Education for the public good where criterion and
outcome guide learning that prepares students to collaborate with others, use
thinking skills to solve problems, and engage productively with society and
its economy, withers when less cost is sufficient for schooling devoted to
individual preference and values antithetical to democracy, social justice, and
principled reasoning.

The values-centric, survival of the fittest, incomplete bottom line ignores the data that indicates how privatization fosters, for instance, lower mathematics achievement. Louisiana, Indiana, Ohio, and Washington, D.C., voucher students earned lower math test scores and these scores stayed lower for at least two years (Barnum, 2019).

Farrie et al. (2019) identify how the incomplete bottom line speaks to legislative abandonment of the responsibility for education. This constitutes a legislature's failure or inability or unwillingness to research the disparities embedded in state funding systems that are less than all students and US democracy deserve.

Without research-based information, solutions for disparities and other funding system problems rarely develop. Challenges "such as developing a cost-based poverty weight, determining strict fiscal capacity to contribute property tax revenue, and allocating additional state revenue to districts with high student need" (Farrie et al., 2019, p. 8) go unaddressed. Less is the evidence that too many legislators stray from their constitutional duty.

Less is embedded in the governance of privatization education. Charter schools, for example, are based on "state-specific charter school authorization statutes—[that] insulate them from direct democratic accountability" (Naclerio, 2017, p. 1159).

Less means that direct accountability to an elected, local, school board is not included on the tiny list of expectations held for privatization education. Path dependence implies that less in the future may include state-sanctioned absentee governance for US schools.

US education cannot be better than the inadequacy of funding directed to instruction. Inadequacy, in this case, derives from the incomplete interpretation of the bottom line for funding education. The long-term effect of the incomplete bottom line is a less effective economy, a less equitable society, and a less vibrant citizenship.

INCOMPLETE AND DIVIDED:
THE BOTTOM LINE FOR US EDUCATION

Education in the United States is split; this wound shows little sign of healing. Bifurcation, the enduring dualities within the theory and practice of US education, ensures that students most in need of quality teaching and learning lack access to it.

Bifurcation, including the divided funding streams that state legislatures manipulate, ensures that insufficient revenue is the norm and not the exception for schools throughout the nation. Bifurcation, carried forward via educational gerrymandering, ensures that an incomplete interpretation of the bottom line of funding separates quality, equity, and adequacy from US schools.

Divided against itself in so many different ways, US education is a wobbly, fraught, enterprise. Instability is inescapable when the intentions of and funding for schools in the United States tug at the intentions and purposes of public education in dramatically different directions. The test that education represents for society reveals the proverbial house divided against itself.

Divided, traditional education is at a standstill and privatization education is a façade. Lip service is given to equity, to "better" as teaching and learning that lead to life success as a common good. But, enactment of fundamentally effective education for all US students cannot emerge when the incomplete bottom line for funding education is dedicated to less. From bifurcation, and from less, students experience only the shadows of dynamic teaching and learning.

To Close the Divide

Ending the dualities that plague US education is "better" worthy of all students and the future of the nation's democracy. Adequate, sufficient, equitable, and fair, teaching and learning in the United States require a restoration of the original power of education (Swensson and Shaffer, 2020). This point of view captures the "better" required if US education is to realize its promises and engage the capabilities of all students.

Advocates for traditional public education point out that quality in teaching and learning (e.g., attaining soft skills, numeracy, artistic proficiency, literacy) avoids "the leveling-down problem whereby equality is achieved by making everyone worse off, without regard for the realization of particular educational goals" (Shields et al., 2017).

The responsibility of education in US democracy and the moral obligation that comes with this responsibility too often go unfulfilled. Aided and abetted by fragmentation, the incomplete interpretation of the bottom line puts students and their futures in limbo.

Negative consequences for individuals, the nation, the economy, and democracy are unavoidable when disparities, gerrymandering, and intentional underfunding are component parts of funding formulas. The incomplete interpretation of the bottom line undersells the capacities that all students bring to public school. This interpretation steals from every classroom. Theft of this magnitude denies the promises of the common good intended by public education. Worse, the incomplete bottom line for funding US education robs the nation of the dynamic instruction without which these promises are out of reach.

Chapter Ten

To Catch a Thief

If the promise and potential of US public education are to be realized, "better" is the next step. If student-centric funding and dynamic instruction are to serve all of US students during the remainder of the twenty-first century, "better" is both a goal and a necessity.

As contemporary state funding formulas, however, abscond with opportunity, equity, and fiscal sufficiency; too many students, school districts, and communities are robbed. Funding formulas are a thief and what's left behind is insufficient for the futures of all US students. The extent to which this thief undercuts teaching and learning throughout US education establishes "better" as a future priority.

"Better," however, is an ironic priority: Nowhere in this discussion is the *best funding* for US public education invoked. The toll taken by the thief in the classroom makes it necessary to establish "better" (student-centric funding for dynamic instruction) before any consideration of education that is best.

The purpose of this chapter is to discuss several non-negotiables for "better" funding of public education in any state. "Better" entails the recognition, first, that conundrums embedded in contemporary funding systems must be resolved.

Next, "better" is sought because the incomplete interpretation of the bottom line for funding public education inhibits revenue derived from criterion and outcome. Finally, "better" is a step beyond reliance on minimums for the role of the public sector.

Embraced within this discussion is the recognition that no single pathway exists for curtailing rampant revenue inequities. This chapter, therefore, will identify representative solutions that can be applied or modified for "better" from state to state. This final chapter is devoted to ending the career of the thief in the classroom.

BIFURCATION: THE CRIMINAL MASTERMIND

If there is a "mastermind" behind theft in the classroom, it is bifurcation. Dualities fostered by bifurcation throughout US education—that is, traditional versus privatization education; vertical versus horizontal equity; cost versus investment; taxpayer equity versus student equity; *accountable-for* versus *accountable-to*—fragment school funding and its effect on teaching and learning. Bifurcation and its attendant dualities ensure that the effects of funding for education correspond with adult-centric teaching and learning.

In the guise of enacting state constitutional language about education, legislatures design and choose the dualities of free market imperatives. Legislatures employ what is known about the extent of the stability or elasticity of taxes (e.g., property, sales, income) to initiate these imperatives and subvert equity.

A License to Steal

In this way, a license to steal from public education is legitimized. Legislative decision-making about educational revenue supports schooling that is excludable and rival. All consequences that arise from theft, as a result, can be written off amid the hubbub of legislative magic as either the cost of doing business or as unintended developments.

The public good of education envisioned in state constitutions, thus, is fragmented. Equitable educational opportunities are shattered. The license to steal supports and extends the exclusion visited on US students by racism and poverty. Research sheds light on this devastating reality.

Baker et al. (2019) found that the average state and local revenues provided to school districts by poverty quintile are flat. The progressivity index for lowest-poverty school districts (0.98) is identical to the index for the highest poverty districts (0.98) (p. 19). "More than two-thirds of states exclude concentrated poverty from their formulas" (Black, 2019, p. 1405).

The Cost that Is Separation

Separation is an enduring cost of decision-making about funding for US education. Instead of collaboration to provide revenue for student-centric teaching and learning, separation is ensured through competition in an adult-centric and amoral marketplace. Where sufficient funding for learning to engage all students with principled reasoning and positive liberty ought to reign, cost avoidance and preference substitution rule instead.

The disconnections endemic to funding formulas are so compelling that, despite insisting that US education should involve less cost, privatization education adherents seek public revenue. True to free market imperatives, this quest forswears public oversight of public funding.

Accessing public dollars while forswearing public governance is the *having your cake while eating it too* facilitated by the license to steal. The license to steal gives life to additional paradoxes including:

- "Instead of a plan to maximize the impact of limited education funding, we have a business model that one charter advocacy group anxiously termed 'a survival of the fittest' supply strategy" (Lafer, 2018, p. 14).
- "Poverty and property taxes are negatively correlated (Baker and Corcoran 2012), resulting in a weaker tax base in poorer, less White neighborhoods" (Weaver and Sosina, 2019, p. 12).
- "One cannot tradeoff spending money on class size reductions against increasing teacher salaries to improve teacher quality if funding is not there for either—if class sizes are already large and teacher salaries non-competitive" (Baker et al., 2016, p. 2).

ENDING THE CLASSROOM CAPER

The thief in the classroom has a head start. Decades of path dependence have entrenched disconnection, misdirection, and ideological alignment in funding systems to the extent that productivity, low-cost, and inequity have become inescapable characteristics of public education.

Ending the caper that robs students of dynamic instruction, professionally trained educators, and challenging and fulfilling instructional programs, necessitates state-specific efforts to tackle conundrums that must be understood to be confronted and confronted to achieve resolution. First, however, a fundamental question must be answered before dealing with two difficult problems facing US public education.

Answering a Fundamental Question

At the core of problem-solving about "better" from future funding formulas of all fifty states lies the answer to this fundamental question: Is it justifiable to create or accept any school funding formula or program from which one group benefits "significantly more in the distribution of resources than others" (Fitzgerald, 2015, p. 59)?

The research base about the importance of funding to answer this question is unequivocal in that there is "consensus among experts and the federal government that low-income students require at least forty percent more resources than the average student" (Black, 2019, p. 1402).

The Effects of an Affirmative Answer

Ideological dedication to less throughout public education leads to an affirmative answer to the fundamental question. When confronted by worrisome research or by court decisions that upend inequitable funding formulas, legislators can justify an affirmative answer to the fundamental question using both lessons learned and legislative magic. Rationalizations derived from lessons and magic assert that the inequities from less are the responsibility of educators and students.

Accepting a funding formula that is the essence of fiscal inequity also is justified when *accountable-to* is riveted to free market theory. The fulfillment of ideological allegiance constitutes justification for funding that advantages one group or locality over others. Policymakers also absolve themselves of *responsible-for* when inequitable funding can be excused by, or blamed on, local effort that fails to fill the gap left by insufficient state revenue.

Ignoring the resource levels required to provide equity, legislatures further undercut students when resources are siphoned away to privatization schools. Less cost, less government, and profiteering undermine the common good. Lee (2018) makes this point succinctly, "the distinct organizational orientation toward profit maximization often becomes incompatible with collective purposes required in publicly offered products and services" (p. 5).

An affirmative answer to the fundamental question ensures that the common good is forsaken. The subversion of the common good puts a priority on the needs of a few to the detriment of "better" for the many.

Under these circumstances, public funding facilitates segregation and state-sponsored discrimination. Moreover, public funding dedicated to the few in privatization schools fails to yield academic proficiency for enrollees beyond achievement levels attained by students in public education (Logan and Burdick-Will, 2015). An affirmative answer to the fundamental question is nothing more than window dressing for ideological purity.

As traditional public schools lose funding to privatization education and as choice education fails to engage all students with "better" teaching and learning, benefits from the equitable distribution of resources are denied to students whose life experience is subject to racism and poverty. In too many states, funding formulas ignore the common good; bifurcated resources sustain inequity and educational opportunity is stolen from US students.

The Effects of a Negative Answer

A negative answer to the fundamental question signals a dramatically different future for US traditional public education. If, for instance, vertical equity and sufficient funding are foundational to a revenue system so that significant educational opportunity is provided to all students, a state's answer to the fundamental question stops both thief and mastermind. This illustration of a legislature's readiness for funding education for the common good depends on resolving two conundrums.

CONUNDRUM 1: THE ROLE OF THE PUBLIC SECTOR

The role of the public sector is linked closely to "generating, claiming, and rationing resources (Schick, 1990). The capacity to budget is determined by how well a government or agency can claim and allocate resources in order to produce specified outcome" (Schick, 1990, as cited in Knoeppel et al., 2013, "Policy Coherence," para. 2). But the dualities endemic to the contemporary role of the public sector and the goal of equitable and sufficient funding for traditional public education are conflicting outcomes.

Legislators and policymakers infuse dualities and disparities throughout US public education. "State school finance systems have evolved to provide lumpy and unpredictable allocations, including through many categorical aid programs intended to provide additional need-based funding for some locations but not others that seem comparably needy" (Baker, 2014, p. 6).

What amounts to an incomplete and counterproductive role given to traditional public education and its funding is captured in "many studies [that] find no difference on average between comparable students who attend charter and non-charter schools" (Braun, Jenkins, & Grigg, 2006; Carnoy, Jacobsen, Mishel, & Rothstein, 2005; NAEP, 2005; Nelson, Rosenberg, and Van Meter, 2004, as cited in Logan and Burdick-Will, 2015, pp. 325–26).

Fragmented funding is wasted; students throughout the United States are ill-served. Adult-centric funding and its dedication to the productivity of a commodity yield the impersonation of education.

Skinner (2019) confirms this baseline and the disparities that blossom from it within US education when she observes that "the state target level of funding per pupil is likely to be influenced by budgetary and other political considerations" (p. 6). Funding formulas are further influenced by ideological outcomes (e.g., mechanisms, efficiency, competition) that are heralded as synonymous with education (Swensson et al., 2019a).

Free market theory and mechanisms treat public education as if it's a Rube Goldberg device. Legislators and privatization education adherents dazzle themselves and others with a celebration of many moving parts without regard for whether these doodads engage all students with the original power of education.

To resolve this first conundrum, an affirmative answer to the fundamental question must be rejected. Resolution of this difficult problem depends on each state's reconsideration of the role of the public sector imposed on traditional public education and supported by contemporary funding systems. No funding system should suffice that ignores or underfunds any group of students to significantly benefit another student group.

The Confrontation Necessary to Resolve this Conundrum

Contemporary public funding for school privatization constitutes a retreat from the common good. This retreat from the common good is the imposition of disconnection on the role of the public sector.

Lee (2018) illuminates the depth of this problem whereby "processes of privatization in education and commodification of schooling fundamentally challenge the two conditions of non-excludability and non-rivalrousness essential to define a public good" (Labaree, 1997; Lubienski, 2006, as cited in Lee, 2018, p. 14).

Existing claims on education and its funding are a combination of business-based efficiency and the pursuit of profit laden with exclusion and rivalry fed by competition. Under the presumption that education is a commodity that ripens ideologically, the potential for the role of the public sector to foster the common good withers. Low-cost individualism is funded and fragmentation denies educational opportunity.

Resolving this conundrum requires a confrontation with impermanence. The now-you-see-it-now-you-don't nature of privatization schooling and its funding constitutes impermanence for learners, for teaching, and for society. Impermanence is an invitation to the minimums that undercut educational opportunity for too many US students.

The role of the public sector in a democracy, always subject to centripetal forces, (e.g., pandemic impacts, cultural divisions) either fosters the resilience required for improvement or ensures the separations embedded in path dependence. Resolution of this first conundrum is linked, also, to understanding and confronting a second serious problem.

CONUNDRUM 2: WHAT IS EDUCATION FOR?

This second conundrum exacerbates the disconnection and misdirection spawned by adult-centric funding. The purpose of US public education becomes a hit-or-miss proposition when dualities and ideology throughout funding formulas distort student-centric ends and means.

Should education focus on job preparation? Should teaching and learning be subjected to ideological imperatives? Should public education live up to the common good and student-centric intentions of state constitutions? The jumble of responses to these and other questions provides confirmation that few have a consistent and reliable notion about the purpose of education.

Even when teaching and learning appear to be the intent of funding formulas, the revenue allocated provides for only minimum outcomes from teaching and learning (Knoeppel et al., 2013; Swensson and Shaffer, 2020). Inequity, inadequacy, and insufficiency suffuse contemporary school funding systems; a quilt-like pattern of less-or-more revenue among and between school districts is the norm instead of the exception (Knoeppel et al., 2013).

Without a clear purpose for education beyond ideology, state legislatures are subject to the winds of political allegiance, the tides of theoretical orthodoxy, and the seismic tremors of legislative leadership when funding systems are designed. Under these conditions, ideological alignment becomes stability. The complexities of quality instructional programs succumb to the ease with which funding-as-theft can be justified when education per se is not the cornerstone of funding foundations.

Student-Centric Funding for Instruction

The resolution for this conundrum is evoked by efforts late in the twentieth and early in the twenty-first centuries to provide adequate funding for instruction. These historic funding reforms demonstrated the positive effect of sufficient revenue on teaching and learning. But these efforts faded or were overturned; little attention is paid in contemporary funding formulas to the positive impact of equitable revenue for dynamic instruction.

Reversing this trend requires the restoration of funding sources and revenue funding levels that lead to previous student-centric impacts in public education. Sufficient student-centric funding dedicated to dynamic instruction for the future can mirror historic achievement levels and the equity in engaged learning that all US students deserve:

- "A 10 percent increase in per-student spending was associated with an increase in low-income students' adult wages by about 7 percent, as well as a 3 percent lower poverty rate" (Partelow et al., 2018, "Money Matters," para. 7).
- "A growing body of high-quality empirical research regarding the importance of equitable and adequate financing for providing high-quality schooling to all children" (Baker 2017; Jackson 2018; Baker 2018, as cited in Baker et al., p. 2) points the way to "better." Vital to this understanding is progressive funding systems that ensure more resources for teaching and learning for students in low-wealth communities and for students with identified learning needs (Baker et al., 2019).
- Researchers report that "the quality of schooling depends largely on the ability of schools or districts to recruit and retain quality employees" (Baker, 2014, p. 8).
- If funding systems ensure that all school districts can pay wages comparable to neighboring districts and comparable to nonteaching jobs in the labor market, then studies demonstrate that quality employees want to be hired and stay in the teaching profession (Baker, 2014; Baker et al., 2016).
- A study of school funding in California indicates that "the evidence suggests that money targeted to students' needs can make a significant difference in student outcomes and can narrow achievement gaps" (Johnson and Tanner, 2018, p. i).

Student-centric education entails funding the instructional engagement of all students with both well-structured and ill-structured problems (Sternberg, 2017). Wisdom, fostered by dynamic instruction linked with the original power of education (Swensson et al., 2019a), makes use of knowledge that is helpful "so long as it's relevant to multiple perspectives and not just to one's own perspective" (Sternberg, 2017).

The Confrontation Necessary to Revolve this Conundrum

To bring student-centric funding and the positive effects of this funding to teaching and learning in US public education requires a confrontation with standardized testing.

Standardized test results present traditional public education with the antithesis of the original power of education because "test scores are imperfect measures of learning and may be weakly linked to adult earnings and success in life" (Jackson et al., 2016, p. 158). Perseverating on outcome accountability ensures that no attention is paid to the heart of learning: dynamic instruction (Swensson and Shaffer, 2020).

The focus on standardized testing in the United States enforces a feedback loop on teaching and learning that renders public education a dizzying whirl of instructional programs glued to lower-order cognition and survival of the fittest. Under these conditions, teachers must "exclude from their lesson plans the material that is not tested in an attempt to maximize the learning opportunity for students on the content of the test" (King and Zucker, 2005, p. 5).

The misdirection fostered throughout US public education by standardized testing means that funding must be redirected to instruction that teaches all students *how to think* (Swensson et al., 2019b). This confrontation pits the importance of engaging all students with the original power of education against contemporary adult-centric funding of education for the exercise of individual, financial, and ideological power. Confrontation for resolution of these two conundrums opens the door to "better" throughout US public education.

LOST POLICIES, ABANDONED DUTY

Abandoned in the contemporary morass that represents revenue for US education is a duty that ought to supersede existing funding priorities. This is the duty of legislatures to provide public education that maximizes the learning opportunities for all students. This duty falls victim to "attempts to contain cost without any basis for knowing or believing that the state has met its constitutional obligations [and] places cost reduction ahead of the state's constitutional duty" (Black, 2019, p. 1427).

The future of teaching and learning during the remainder of the twenty-first century depends on reasserting duty for the common good within legislative policy. Ending the split personality of education in the United States to ensure equitable and sufficient funding demands that the nation recover:

- Citizen involvement throughout schooling to re-establish public governance for every school receiving public funds.
- Safeguards for the rights of all students who attend any school funded by public revenue that is created by state law, rule, or administrative fiat. Existing legal and moral safeguards for the rights of all students cannot be abridged by attendance or enrollment in any school funded by public dollars (Baker and Miron, 2015).
- Confirmation that publicly funded education is incompatible with outcome accountability and deregulation, the cornerstones of privatization. Yet privatization education continues to be funded by tax dollars and by tax funding masquerading as "scholarships" and other forms of tax evasion.

- Funding for public education is locked in a policy loop that permits little flexibility and less recognition of the purpose of teaching and learning for the remainder of the twenty-first century. Moreover, thinking about funding for schooling in the US circles around tracking revenue instead of expenditures (Wolf et al., 2014). Revenue, as a total dollar amount received, creates an artificial gap that privatization proponents exploit to illustrate the allegation of funding inequities.
- The per-pupil revenue gap between traditional public education and privatization education ($3,814 according to Wolf et al., 2014) is never explained in terms that differentiate funding for non-instructional costs including facilities, transportation, insurance, utilities, and maintenance that are tallied in most state and local funding for traditional public schools. More to the point of a focus on teaching and learning because traditional public schools welcome and serve all students, increased costs for personnel who educate English-language learners, special needs students, and homeless students are not described or tallied when ROI revenue comparisons are made.

Listening to Whispers: What Reform of *Minimum* Funding Tells Us

States attempted to establish "better" in public education through funding reform. But SFRs were short-lived. The voices that speak to those successes are now little more than whispers. Nevertheless, the story of the positive impact of sufficient funding, turning away from funding formulas for *the minimum*, must be amplified to empower a future of funding equity and dynamic instruction. Several examples speak loudly to the student-centric impact of sufficient instructional revenue.

Past examples reveal that "money infused through school finance reforms, which led to higher salaries and smaller classes, did in fact lead to improved outcomes" (Baker, 2016, p. 13). Research about funding use in Texas indicates that "teacher expertise (measured by teacher experience, education, and certification examination scores) was the most powerful predictor of student achievement" (Darling-Hammond, 2019, p. 7).

A 1992 court decision (*Hancock v. Driscoll*) led to the Education Reform Act in Massachusetts that not only put in place a weighted formula for students in low-wealth districts that sought to equalize state funding and local effort but also included "new standards and assessments demanding more intellectually ambitious teaching and learning" (Darling-Hammond, 2019, p. 13).

These examples rarely serve as inspiration for contemporary funding formulas. But during the first two decades of the twenty-first century some states have made an investment to support higher-order thinking and dynamic instruction.

NAEP score improvements in Connecticut, for example, reflect an alignment of sufficient and equitable resources with dynamic instruction. Connecticut "provided targeted resources to the neediest districts, including funding for professional development for teachers and administrators, preschool and all-day kindergarten for students, and smaller pupil-teacher ratios" (Darling-Hammond, 2019, p. 10).

New Hampshire, also, "has been transforming its curriculum and assessment system to focus more intently on higher order thinking and performance skills and investing in professional learning for educators" (Darling-Hammond, 2019, p.8). The result of this investment is New Hampshire's third-in-the-nation best NAEP scores for 2017 in both Reading and Mathematics at the eighth grade.

Dynamic instruction requires real resources (e.g., staffing, materials, services) and dynamic instruction requires specialized resources to meet the learning needs of students in poverty, English-language learners, or students with special needs. These resources include but are not limited to "smaller class sizes and other resource-intensive interventions [that] may be required to strive for those outcomes commonly achieved by the state's average child" (Baker et al., 2016, p. 6).

Scholars summarized the effect of *sufficient* funding: "achievement scores from U.S. school districts with substantial funding and low student poverty are similar to those earned by the highest-scoring countries in international comparative studies" (Biddle and Berliner, 2002, p. 60).

Scholars, moreover, indicate the impact of *sufficient, equitable, funding*: "rigorous empirical literature has validated that state school finance reforms can have substantive, positive effects on student outcomes, including reductions in outcome disparities or increases in overall outcome levels" (Baker et al., 2016, p. 4).

DUTY, OPPORTUNITY, AND SUFFICIENCY

Various factors aid and abet the thief in the classroom. The FDZ, *accountable-to*, and preference substitution are among the factors that render funding for US education adult-centric. Restricting the role of the public sector to minimums while permitting gerrymandered funding formulas, legislatures ensure that US public education cannot escape the dire consequences of path dependence and inequitable and insufficient funding.

The mantra of less-cost-less-government imposes additional negative consequences. Public schools are among the last functioning civic organizations in the lives of many US citizens (Swensson and Shaffer, 2020). The reality of less government at less cost means traditional public schools often provide health care services, nutrition for students and their families, child care before and after school, or other interventions for public health and student safety.

Overburdened and underfunded, public educators scramble to cobble together partnerships and networks that can deliver these services to students and their families. No additional revenue from funding formulas arrives as traditional public schools are stretched well beyond the constitutional intention for state-provided education.

The less-is-more role of the public sector envisioned by free market theory underfunds *and* overwhelms traditional public education. Insufficient funding ensures that educational opportunity is limited. Insufficient government ensures that the common good of readily available public services is limited.

A Future Choice

Under these circumstances, student-centric public education becomes a future choice possible only if funding is aligned with duty, opportunity, and sufficiency. Legislatures, first, must invest in the permanence of duty to traditional public education. The exercise of this duty to all students throughout a state does not, and cannot, survive the impermanence of bifurcation rooted in contemporary funding formulas. This constitutional duty is fulfilled permanently when all students are the purpose of traditional public education and its funding.

Opportunity for all students, not some, is an obligation finally fulfilled by public education if the duty of a legislature to provide funding sufficient to educational opportunity for all is undertaken permanently, free from the malign influence of ideological imperatives and bifurcation.

Dualities justified by survival of the fittest and fueled by new public management guarantee that opportunity to learn is placed beyond the reach of many students. In the absence of opportunity and funding sufficient to robust engagement with dynamic instruction, poverty and racism thrive.

FUNDING IS A CHOICE: SOCIETY OR IDEOLOGY?

Funding for US public education is a choice. Will legislatures, policymakers, and citizens tolerate the continuation of educational bifurcation and insufficiency? Or will decision-makers and voters choose to journey toward equity and dynamic instruction. Making this choice will determine how the nation responds to the test of education. How the United States sees itself during the remainder of the twenty-first century hangs in the balance.

The charade perpetrated by insufficiencies and underfunding created by contemporary funding formulas and the ideology that supports these systems ensures that too many students experience teaching and learning that leaves them ill-equipped for life success. Ending the terrible price paid by students (and consequently paid by the nation) when funding chaos yields under-achievement depends on the elimination of revenue fragmentation.

Funding formulas for the future must be evolving hybrids riveted to criterion and outcome that are student-centric and driven by sufficiency instead of minimums. Funding levels devoid of any connection with standardized testing and engaged by specified educational thresholds are essential to the common good as the purpose of traditional public education.

The common good of dynamic instruction evokes teaching and learning as the interaction between intelligences necessary for engagement with *how to think*. Sternberg (2017) sheds light on this threshold within his description of

> wise thinking as that which seeks a common good by balancing one's own interests with other people's and with larger interests, over the long as well as the short term, through the use of positive ethical values (Baker 2017; Jackson 2018; Baker 2018, as cited in Sternberg, 2017, "More than one way to think," para. 1).

CHOOSING INTERDEPENDENCE: FUNDING EDUCATION ON BEHALF OF SOCIETY

Educational disparities are fostered by the separations and dualities endemic to contemporary school funding systems. The common good of student-centric teaching and learning, as a result, lies in pieces across society. Inter-dependence is the equivalent of society's super glue if public education and the common good are to be reconnected.

Legislatures must interweave criterion and outcome in a student-centric foundation for public education and its funding. Such a foundation could incorporate the view that education "requires a balance of creativity, intelligence, and wisdom: creativity to generate new ideas, intelligence to vet the quality of the ideas, and wisdom to ensure that the ideas serve a common good" (Sternberg, 2003, as cited in Sternberg, 2017, "Why does it all matter?" para. 5).

Interdependent with this vision of what public education must become is the duty of each legislature to establish funding sufficient to and equitable for dynamic instruction that fulfills the promise represented by Sternberg's view. A focus on the interdependence between a legislature's duty and re-sponsibility for student-centric traditional public education can occur when legislatures compare how much their state actually "spends to how much *it would have to spend* for its students to achieve a common goal" (Baker et al., 2019, p. 9).

Interdependence also is missing from contemporary funding formulas because sufficiency and progressivity are treated as disconnected aspects of school finance. As Baker et al. (2019) suggest, establishing interdependence between progressivity and sufficiency is a baseline from which education is an investment in both students and society.

To Advance Interdependence

The advance of interdependence can begin with legislative action aligned with a 2017 statement from the NAACP: "While high-quality, accountable, and accessible charters can contribute to educational opportunity, by them-selves, even the best charters are not a substitute for more stable, adequate and equitable investments in public education" (Brown, 2017). The reason for enacting interdependent school funding on behalf of US society is clear:

> As research continues to document, the racial/ethnic achievement gap is per-sistent and large in the US and has lasting labor market effects, whereby the achievement gap has been found to explain a significant part of racial/ethnic income disparities (Reardon, Robinson-Cimpian, & Weathers 2015, as cited in Shields et al., 2017).

Contemporary disparities and dualities embedded in funding for US pub-lic education represents a failure of US society to see beyond the present. The disconnections engendered by the frenzy for less educational cost are a myopia unable to envision the economic and social costs of poverty, racism, incarceration, low-wage employment, and economic malaise.

These costs are paid when student-centric public education is subsumed by funding inequities that foster incomplete teaching and learning. The in-sistence of ideologues and policymakers on creating fragmented revenue as if underfunded education can be equitable ensures that the promises of US public education are fulfilled only for the most privileged.

The long-range cost to US society is overwhelming. "Literature has led researchers to conclude that equal access to quality schools remains a large source of the racial and ethnic gaps in academic achievement" (Card & Roth-stein, 2007; Orfield & Yun, 1999, as cited in Logan and Burdick-Will, 2015, p. 324). Funding to purchase a commodity in an amoral market ensures "that profitable services are not designed to bring advantages to all students" (Lee, 2018, p. 13).

Without a focus on interdependence to generate sufficient funding for dynamic instruction, the capabilities and futures of all US students are stolen. To nab the thief in the classroom requires choosing an ongoing interdependence between legislative duty and sufficient funding for educational opportunity for all US students.

The end of bifurcation of funding, and the adoption public funding systems solely dedicated to traditional public education, is the baseline for *sufficient funding formulas* (SFFs). Baker and Corcoran (2012) articulate this interdependent future funding for US education when they note that scholars "argue that horizontal and vertical equity can effectively be folded into a single concept of equal educational opportunity, where the equity object of interest is the desired student outcome goal" (p. 15).

Educational opportunity depends on the realization that traditional public education exists for the common good. US students deserve SFFs that provide solely for traditional public education. To catch the thief and end the damage done to students when dynamic instruction is stolen by underfunding, policymakers and legislators must fulfill duty instead of embracing ideology.

Adult-centric funding systems rationalized by *accountable-to* must be jettisoned. In place of the ineffectual funding status quo, equitable and sufficient funding for traditional public education becomes the "better" for student-centric instruction that is the ultimate, best, investment for the US future.

References

Altemus, V. (2010, May 5). *Review of "They Spend WHAT? The Real Cost of Public Schools."* Boulder, CO and Tempe, AZ: Education and the Public Interest Center & Education Policy Research Unit. Retrieved from http://epicpolicy.org/thinktank /review-they-spend-what.

American Federation of Teachers (AFT). (2018). *A Decade of Neglect Public Education Funding in the Aftermath of the Great Recession.* Washington, DC: American Federation of Teachers.

Atchison, D. (2019). Forgotten Equity: The Promise and Subsequent Dismantling of Education Finance Reform in New York State. *Education Policy Analysis Archives (27)*143. Retrieved from https://doi.org/10.14507/epaa.27.4422.

Augenblick, J. G., Myers, J. L., and Anderson, A. B. (1997, Winter). Equity and Adequacy in School Funding: The Future of Children. *Financing Schools (7)*3.

Baker, B. D. (2014, July). *America's Most Financially Disadvantaged School Districts and How They Got that Way.* Washington, DC: Center for American Progress.

————. (2016, May). *Review of School Spending and Student Achievement in Michigan. What's the Relationship?* Boulder, CO: National Education Policy Center. Retrieved from http://nepc.colorado.edu/thinktank/review-school-spending.

————. (2019, April). The Adequacy and Fairness of State School Finance Systems. *School Finance Indicators Database.* Newark, NJ: Albert Shanker Institute, Rutgers Graduate School of Education. Retrieved from https://files.eric.ed.gov /fulltext/ED606197

Baker, B. D., and Corcoran, S. P. (2012). *The Stealth Inequities of School Funding: How State and Local School Finance Systems Perpetuate Inequitable Student Spending.* Washington, DC: Center for American Progress.

Baker, B. D., and Miron, G. (2015, December). *The Business of Charter Schooling: Understanding the Policies that Charter Operators Use for Financial Benefit.* Boulder, CO: National Education Policy Center. Retrieved from http://nepc.colo rado.edu/publication/charter-revenue.

Baker, B. D., and Weber, M. (2016). State School Finance Inequities and the Limits of Pursuing Teacher Equity through Departmental Regulation. *Education Policy Analysis Archives (24)*47, 1–36. Retrieved from http://dx.doi.org/10.14507/epaa.v24.2230.

Baker, B. D., DiCarlo, M., and Weber, M. (2019). *The Adequacy and Fairness of State School Finance Systems. Findings from the School Finance Indicators Database, School Year 2015–2016.* Washington, DC: Albert Shanker Institute. Retrieved from www.schoolfinancedata.org.

Baker, B. D., Farrie, D., and Sciarra, D. G. (2016). *Mind the Gap: 20 Years of Progress and Retrenchment in School Funding and Achievement Gaps.* (Policy Information Report and ETS Research Report Series No. RR-16-15). Princeton, NJ: Education Testing Service. doi:10.1002/ets2.12098.

Baker, B. D., Libby, K., and Wiley, K. (2012). *Spending by the Major Charter Management Organizations: Comparing Charter School and Local Public District Financial Resources in New York, Ohio, and Texas.* Boulder, CO: National Education Policy Center. Retrieved from http://nepc.colorado.edu/publication/spending-major-charter

Barnum, M. (2017, June 12). Why for-profit charter schools are going out of style with some education leaders. *Chalkbeat.* Retrieved from www.chalkbeat.org/matt.barnum.page40

———. (2019, April 23). Do voucher students' scores bounce back after initial declines? New evidence says no. *Chalkbeat.* Retrieved from www.chalkbeat.org/matt.barnum.page17

Berkshire, J. C. (2019, December 30). The Democrats' School Choice Problem. *The Nation.* Retrieved from www.thenation.com with https://www.thenation.com/article/archive/education-school-choice-democrats/

Biddle, B. J., and Berliner, D. C. (2002, May). Research Synthesis/Unequal Funding in the United States. *Educational Leadership (59)*8, 48–59.

Black, D. W. (2019, December). Educational Gerrymandering: Money, Motives, and Constitutional Rights. *New York University Law Review (94)*6, 1385–464.

Born, C. (2020). *Making Sense of School Finance: A Practical State-by-State Approach.* London: Rowman and Littlefield.

Boser, U., Boser, M., and Roth, E. (2018, March 20) *The Highly Negative Impact of Vouchers.* Washington, DC: Center for American Progress.

Brimley, V., Jr., Verstegen, D. A., and Garfield, R. R. (2012). *Financing Education in a Climate of Change* (11th ed.). Upper Saddle River, NJ: Pearson Education, Inc.

Brown v. Board of Education, 347 U.S. 483(1954).

Brown, E. (2017, July 26). Choice not the answer to improving education for black students. *The Washington Post.* Retrieved from https://www.washingtonpost.com/local/education/naacp-school-choice-is-not-the-answer-to-improving-education-for-black-students/2017/07/26/7b4edcf0-721c-9eac-d56bd5568db8_story.

Bruecker, E. (2017). *Assessing the Fiscal Impact of Wisconsin's Statewide Voucher Program.* Boulder, CO: National Education Policy Center.

Bruno, P. (2019, May). *Charter Competition and District Finances: Evidence from California Students.* (PACE Working Paper). University of Southern California: Rossier School of Education.

Carden, D. (2009, December 16). Gov. Daniels to Cut $300 Million from Schools. *NWI Times,* Munster, IN.

Carlson, D. E., Cowen, J. M., and Fleming, D. J. (2013). Third-Party Governance and Performance Measurement: A Case Study of Publicly Funded Private School Vouchers. *Journal of Public Administration Research and Theory (25),* 897–922. doi:10.1093/jopart/mut017.

Chingos, M. M., and Blagg, K. (2017, November). *Making Sense of State School Funding Policy.* (Research Report). Washington, DC: Urban Institute.

Coffin, S., and Cooper, B. S. (2016). *Sound School Finance for Educational Excellence.* London: Rowman & Littlefield.

Combs, A., Foster, J., and Toma, E. F. (2018). Local Responses to School Finance Equalization: Wealth or Place? *Public Finance and Management (18)*3/4, 224–50.

Corcoran, S., Romer, T., and Rosenthal, H. (2017). The Twilight of the Setter? Public School Budgets in a Time of Institutional Change. *Economics and Politics (29),* 1–21. doi:10.1111/ecpo.12087.

Cubberley, E. P. (1905). *School funds and their appointment: A consideration of the subject with reference to a more general equalization of both the burdens and the advantages of education.* New York: Teachers College, Columbia University.

Darling-Hammond, L. (2019). *Investing for student success: Lessons from state school finance reforms.* Palo Alto, CA: Learning Policy Institute.

DeAngelis, C., Wolf, P., Maloney, L., and May, J. (2019, April). *A Good Investment: The Updated Productivity of Public Charter Schools in Eight U.S. Cities.* (School Choice Demonstration Project). Fayetteville: University of Arkansas. Retrieved from http://www.uaedreform.org/a-good-investment-public-charter-schools-in -8-us-cities.

DeAngelis, C. A., Wolf, P. J., Maloney, L. D., and May, J. F. (2018, November). *Charter School Funding: (More) Inequity in the City.* (School Choice Demonstration Project). Fayetteville: University of Arkansas. Retrieved from http://www .uaedreform.org/charter-school-funding-more-inequity-in-the-city.

Dynarksi, M. (2016, May 26). *On Negative Effects of Vouchers.* (Evidence Speaks Reports [1]18). Washington, DC: Brookings Institute, Center on Children and Families.

Education Week. (2020, April 17). *50 Years Seeking Educational Equality: Revisiting the Coleman Report.* Retrieved from www.edweek.org.

Ellis, L. D. (2010). *A Call to Leadership: The First Fifty Years of the Indiana Association of Public School Superintendents.* West Lafayette, IN: Purdue University Press.

Farrie, D. (2018, July). *Trenton Public Schools: Budget Impacts of Underfunding and Rapid Charter Growth.* (Report). Newark, NJ: Education Law Center.

Farrie, D., Kim, R., and Sciarra, D. (2019). *Making the Grade 2019: How Fair Is School Funding in Your State?* (Report). Newark, NJ: Education Law Center.

Feuerstein, A., and Henry, S. E. (2020, June 3). Betsy DeVos Is Looting Public Schools. *Newsweek.* Retrieved from www.newsweek.com/feuersteinandhenry

Fiddiman, B., and Yin, J. (2019). *The Danger Private School Voucher Programs Pose to Civil Rights.* (Report). Washington, DC: Center for American Progress.

Fischer, B. (2013, January 3). ALEC's Schoolhouse Rock. *The Progressive.* Retrieved from www.progressive.org.

Fittes, E. K. (2020, May 28). Holcomb applied for $61m in relief for schools. Here are 3 things to know. *ChalkBeat.* Retrieved from https://in.chalkbeat.org/2020/5/28/21273933/holcomb-applied-for-61m-in-relief-for-schools-here-are-3-things-to-know.

Fitzgerald, R. (2015). Philosophy Rather than Finance: Redirecting the Discourse Concerning Inequitable School Funding in Illinois. *Philosophical Studies in Education (46)*, 52–61.

Ford, M. R. (2016, Winter). Funding Impermanance: Quantifying the Public Funds Sent to Closed Schools in the Nation's First Urban School Voucher Program. *Public Administration Quarterly (40)*4, 882–912.

Fraser-Burgess, S. (2012). Group Identity: Deliberative Democracy, and Diversity in Education. *Educational Philosophy and Theory (44)*5, 480–501. doi: 10.1111/j.1469-5812.2010.00717.x

Friedman, M. (1955). The Role of Government in Education. In: Robert A. Solo, ed., *Economics and the Public Interest*, 123–144. New Brunswick, NJ: Rutgers University Press. Retrieved from https://miltonfriedman.hoover.org/objects/58044//the-role-of-government-in-education.

Gallo, Jr., P. J. (2014). Reforming the "Business" of Charter Schools in Pennsylvania. *B.Y.U. Education and Law Review (2014)*2, 206–32. Retrieved from https://digitalcommons.law.byu/elj/vol2014/iss2/3.

Gilblom, E. A., and Sang, H. I. (2019). Closure and the Roles of Student Performance and Enrollment Characteristics: A Survival Analysis of Charter Schools in Ohio's Largest Urban Counties. *Education Policy Analysis Archives (27)*107, 1–36. Retrieved from https://doi.org/10.14507/epaa.27.4568.

Girardi-Schachter, T. (2019, September 2). Top 10 States for Manufacturing 2019. *Global Trade.* Retrieved from www.globaltrademag.com.

Goldstein, D. (2015). *The Teacher Wars: A History of America's Most Embattled Profession.* New York: Anchor Books.

Greene, P. (2019a, March 29). Report: The Department of Education Has Spent $1 Billion on Charter School Waste and Fraud. *Forbes.* Retrieved from https://google.com/amp/s/forbes.com/sites/petergreene/report-the-department-of-education-has-spent-1-billion-on-charter-school-waste-and-fraud.

———. (2019b, June 13). If the Supreme Court Hears This Case, It Could Change the Face of Public Education. *Forbes.* Retrieved from www.forbes.com.

Hankins-Diaz, E. (2016). Is it Really a Choice? How Charter Schools Without Choice May Result in Students Without a Free Appropriate Public Education. *B.Y.U. Education & Law Journal (2016)*1, 25–72.

Hanushek, E. A. (2016, Spring). What Matters for Student Achievement: Updating Coleman on the Influence of Families and Schools. *Education Next (16)*2, 1–11.

———. (2020). The Unavoidable: Tomorrow's Teacher Compensation. *(Policy Analysis).* Stanford, CA: The Hoover Institute.

Hanushek, E. A., Ruhose, J., and Woessmann, L. (2016, Summer). It Pays to Improve School Quality: States that Boost Student Achievement Could Reap Large Economic Gains. *Education Next (16)*3. Retrieved from www.go.gale.com/hanushek.ruhose.woessmann

Herron, A. (2020, Jan 16). Some, But Not All Indiana Districts Gave Teachers Pay Raises for the Last School Year. *The Indianapolis Star.* Retrieved from https://www.indystar.com/story/news/education/2020/01/16/indiana-teacher-pay-2018-2019-school-year-salaries-2733108001.

Hicks, M. (2019, June 17). Opinion: My Talk to School Superintendents. *DuBois County Free Press.* Retrieved from www.duboiscountyfreepress.com/opinion-my-talk-to-school-superintendents.

Indiana Constitution. (1851). *Constitution of the State of Indiana Article 8, Section 1.* As amended 2016. Retrieved from www.law/indiana.edu; www.iga.in.gov.

Jackson, C. K., Johnson, R. C., and Persico, C. (2016). The Effects of School Spending on Educational and Economic Outcomes: Evidence from School Finance Reforms. *The Quarterly Journal of Economics,* 157–218. doi:10.1093/qje/qjv036.

Jackson, R. (2020, February 23). Commentary: Holcomb, GOP Undermine Public Education. *Indiana Economic Digest.* Bloomington, IN: HeraldTimesOnline. Retrieved from https://indianaeconomicdigest.com/Content/Most-Recent/Education/Article/COMMENTARY-Holcomb-GOP-undermine-public-education/31/77/98927.

Johnson, J. L., and Vesely, R. S. (2017). Equity and Adequacy in Ohio School Funding. *Leadership and Research in Education (4)*1, 90–105.

Johnson, R. C., and Tanner, S. (2018). Money and Freedom: The Impact of California's School Finance Reform on Academic Achievement and the Composition of District Spending. *(Technical Report).* Policy Analysis for California Education (PACE): Stanford University.

Jung, Y. (2018). Economic Discussion of Conflict between Public Education Policies and Common Good Arts in the United States. *The Journal of Arts Management, Law, and Society (48)*2, 98–107. Retrieved from http://dx.doi.org/10,1080.106329 21.2017.1303412.

Kids Count. (2020). *Indiana Kids Count Data Book.* Indianapolis: Indiana Youth Institute. Retrieved from www.datacenter.kidscount.org.

King, K. V., and Zucker, S. (2005, August). Curriculum Narrowing. *(Policy Report).* London: Pearson.

Kitzmiller, E. M. (2019, Spring). Public Schools, Private Dollars: An Education Arms Race. *Phi Kappa Phi Forum (99)*1, 14–17.

Knoeppel R., Pitts, D. A., and Lindle, J. C. (2013). *Taxation and Education: Using Educational Research to Inform Coherent Policy for the Public Good.* Clemson, SC: Clemson University TigerPrints. Retrieved from https://tigerprints.clemson.edu/eugene_pubs.

Knoeppel, R. C., and Rinehart, J. S. (2008). Explaining the Relationship between Resources and Student Achievement: A Methodological Comparison of Production Functions and Canonical Analysis. *Educational Considerations (35)*2, 29–40.

Kogan, V., Lavertu, S., and Peskowitz, Z. (2016, April). Performance Federalism and Local Democracy: Theory and Evidence from School Tax Referenda. *American Journal of Political Science (60)*2, 418–435. doi:10.1111/ajps.12184.

Koller, K., and Welsch, D. M. (2017). Location Decisions of Charter Schools: An Examination of Michigan. *Education Economics (25)*2, 158–82. Retrieved from http://dx.doi.org/10.1080/09645292.2016.1203866.

Ladd, H. F., and Singleton, J. (2018). Charter school growth puts fiscal pressure on Traditional Public Schools. *Brown Center Chalkboard.* Retrieved from www .brookings.edu/blog.2018/05/01

———. (2019). The Fiscal Externalities of Charter Schools: Evidence from North Carolina. *Education Finance and Policy (15)*1. Retrieved from https://doi.org /10.1162/edfp_a_00272.

Ladd, H. F., Clotfelter, C. T., and Turaeva, M. (2018, June). Choosing Charter Schools in North Carolina: What Do Parents Value? (CALDER Working Paper No. 196-0618-1). Washington, DC: National Center for Analysis of Longitudinal Data in Education Research.

Lafer, G. (2018). Breaking Point: The Cost of Charter Schools for Public School Districts. (Report). Washington, DC: In the Public Interest. Retrieved from www .inthepublicinterest.org.

Lake, R., Jochim, A., Hill, P., and Tuchman, S. (2019, May). *Do Charter Schools Cause Fiscal Distress in School Districts?* (Brief). Bothell, WA: Center on Reinventing Public Education.

Larkin, B. (2016). Funding Students, Not Units: Moving Alabama from a Regressive Public School Funding State to a Progressive School Funding State. *Alabama Journal of Educational Leadership (3)*, 15–37.

Larkin B., and Weiler, S. C. (2017, Winter). Making Sense of Fiscal Uncertainty: An Overview of the 2016 State of the States. *Journal of Education Finance (42)*3, 243–46.

Leachman, M., Masterson, K., Fiqueroa, E. (2017, November 29). A Punishing Decade for School Funding. (Analysis). Washington, DC: Center for Budget and Policy Priorities. Retrieved from https://www.cbpp.org/sites/default/files/atoms /files/11-29-17sfp.pdf.

Lee, J. (2004). How Feasible Is Adequate Yearly Progress (AYP)? Simulations of School AYP, 'Uniform Averaging' and 'Safe Harbor' under the No Child Left Behind Act. *Education Policy Analysis Archives (12)*14, 1–19. Retrieved from http:// epaa.asu.edu/epaa/v12n13/.

———. (2018). Understanding Site Selection of For-Profit Educational Management Organization Charter Schools. *Education Policy Analysis Archives (26)*77, 3–17. Retrieved from http://dx.doi.org/10.14507/epaa.26.3024.

Lepore, J. (2018). *These Truths: A History of the United States.* New York: W. W. Norton & Company.

Levin, H. Y. (2013). Tax Credit Scholarship Programs and the Changing Ecology of Public Education. *Arizona State Law Journal (45)*1033, 1051–75.

Lifto, D., and Nicol, B. (2019). *School Tax Elections: Planning for Success in the New Normal*, 3rd ed. London: Rowman & Littlefield.

Lindsay, J. (2018, July 20). Indiana Education Funding Not Back to Pre-Recession Levels. *News Education.* Retrieved from www.Wfyi.org.

Logan, J. R., and Burdick-Will, J. (2015). School Segregation, Charter Schools, and Access to Quality Education. *Journal of Urban Affairs (38)*3, 323-43. doi:10.1111/juaf.12246.

Lubienski, C. (2013). Privatising Form or Function? Equity, Outcomes, and Influence in American Charter Schools. *Oxford Review of Education (39)*4, 498–513. Retrieved from http://dx.doi.org/10.1080/03054985.2013.821853.

Malinowski, M. (2014). *The Mystery in School Finances: Discovering Answers in Community-Based Budgeting.* London: Rowman and Littlefield.

Martin, C., Boser, U., Benner, M., and Baffour, P. (2018, November 13). *A Quality Approach to School Funding: Lessons Learned from School Finance Litigation.* Washington, DC: Center for American Progress. Retrieved from www.americanprogress.org.

McFarland, J., Hussar, B., Zhang, J., Wang, X., Wang, K., Hein S., . . . Barmer, A. (2019). *The Condition of Education 2019 (NCES 2019-144).* U.S. Department of Education. Washington, DC: National Center for Education Statistics. Retrieved from https://nces.ed.gov/pubsearch/pubsinfo.asp?pubid=2019144.

Miksza, K., Robinson, J., and Schlegel-Ruegger, M. (2019). *Over 99% of Indiana Voucher Money Goes to Religious Schools.* BLOG. Bloomington, IN: Indiana Coalition for Public Education (ICPE), Monroe County. Retrieved from www.icpe-monroecounty.org.

Minorini, P. A., and Sugarman, S. D. (1999). Educational Adequacy and the Courts: The Promise and Problems of Moving to a New Paradigm. In: H. F. Ladd, R. Chalk, and J. S. Hansen, Eds., *Equity and Adequacy in Education Finance Issues and perspectives*, 175–208. Washington, DC: National Academy Press.

Molnar, A., Miron, G., Elgeberi, N., Barbour, M. K., Huerta, L., Shafer, S. R., and Rice, J. K. (2019). *Virtual Schools in the U.S. 2019.* Boulder, CO: National Education Policy Center. Retrieved from http://nepc.colorado.edu/publication/virtual-schools-annual-2019.

Moon, J. S., and Stewart, M. S. (2016, October). Understanding How School Vouchers Are Funded: Summary of Funding for the Indiana Choice Scholarship Program. Research Brief: Center for Evaluation & Education Policy (CEEP). Bloomington, IN: Indiana University School of Education.

Morgan, I., and Amerikaner, A. (2018, February). *Funding Gaps: Too Many Students Do Not Get Their Fair Share of Education Funding.* Washington, DC: The Education Trust. Retrieved from https://edtrust.org/wp-content/uploads/2014/09/FundingGapReport_2018_FINAL.pdf.

Mort, P. R., and Ruesser, W. C. (1951). *Public School Finance: Its Background, Structure, and Operation.* New York: McGraw-Hill Book Company, Inc.

Naclerio, M. A. (2017). Accountability through Procedure? Rethinking Charter School Accountability and Special Education Rights. *Columbia Law Review (117)*, 1153–90.

National Center for Educational Statistics (NCES). (n.d.). US Department of Education. Retrieved from www.2.ed.gov.

National Commission on Excellence in Education. (1983). *A Nation at Risk: The Imperative for Educational Reform.* Washington, DC: United States Department of Education.

National Education Association (NEA). (n.d.). *Why Cultural Competence?* Retrieved from www.nea.org.

National Law Review. (2020, June 30). Supreme Court Decides *Espinoza v. Montana Department of Revenue. National Law Review (X)*202. Retrieved from https://www.natlawreview.com/article/supreme-court-decides-espinoza-v-montana-department-revenue

Nelson, A. A., and Balu, R. (2014). Local Government Responses to Fiscal Stress: Evidence from the Public Education Sector. *Public Administration Review (74)*5, 601–14. doi:10.1111/puar.12211.

Palardy, J., Nesbit, T. M., and Adzima, K. A. (2015). Charter versus Traditional Public Schools: A Panel Study of the Technical Efficiency in Ohio. *Education Economics (23)*3, 278–95. Retrieved from http://dx.doi.org/10.1080/09645292.2012.748014.

Partelow, L., Shapiro, S., McDaniels, A., and Brown, C. (2018, September 20) *Fixing Chronic Disinvestment in K–12 Schools.* Washington, DC: Center for American Progress.

Penn State. (2019). *The Price of Standardized Testing.* Education: Just Another Sites at Penn State site. Retrieved from www.sites.pennstate.edu.

Picchi, A. (2018, Sep 5). Teachers' Wage Penalty Is at a Record High. *CBS News.* Retrieved from https://www.cbsnews.com/news/teachers-wage-penalty-is-at-a-record-high.

Powell, O. E. (1933). *Educational Returns at Varying Expenditure Levels.* New York: Bureau of Publications, Teachers College Columbia University.

Public Funds Public Schools (PFPS). (2019a, Nov 26). Private School Vouchers: Analysis of 2019 State Legislative Sessions. Retrieved from www.pfps.org.

———. (2019b, Dec 4). Private School Vouchers: Continued Bipartisan Opposition in Georgia and Arkansas. Retrieved from www.pfps.org.

———. (2020a, Feb 27). While Public Schools Suffer, New York State Sends over $250 Million to Private Schools. Retrieved from www.pfps.org.

———. (2020b, Mar 2). Parents Sue Tennessee to Block Unconstitutional Voucher Law. Retrieved from www.pfps.org .

Ravitch, D. (2020, July 20). The Coronavirus Just Might End School Privatization Nonsense. *Education Week.* Retrieved from www.edweek.org.

Rentner, D. S. (2019). Are Public School Teachers Adequately Compensated? (Report). Washington, DC: Center on Education Policy.

Rogers, R. (2015). Making Public Policy: The New Philanthropists and American Education. *American Journal of Economics and Sociology (74)*4, 743–44. doi:10.1111/ajes.12113.

Rowe, R. K. (2010, Summer). Beyond Equality and Adequacy: Equal Protection, Tax Assessments, and the Missouri Public School Funding Dilemma. *Missouri Law Review (75)*3, 1037–66.

Sass, T. R., Zimmer, R. W., Gill, B. P., and Booker T. K. (2016). Charter High Schools' Effects on Long-Term Attainment and Earnings. *Journal of Policy Analysis and Management (35)*3, 683–706. doi: 10.1002/pam.21913.

Savransky, R. (2017, May 17). DeVos: School Choice Opponents Are "Flat Earthers." *The Hill.* Retrieved from www.thehill.com.

Scafidi, B. (2016, Winter). The Dismal Productivity Trend for K–12 Public Schools and How to Improve It. *Cato Journal (36)*1.

Schneider, J. (2019, May 30). Charter Schools Were Supposed to Save Public Education. Why Did People Turn on Them? *The Washington Post.* Retrieved from http://www.washingtonpost.com.

Schwenkenberg, J., and Vanderhoff, J. (2015). Why Do Charter Schools Fail? An Analysis of Charter School Survival in New Jersey. *Contemporary Economic Policy (33)*2, 300–14. doi:10.1111/coep.12068.

Shaffer, M. B., and Dincher, B. (2020). In Indiana, School Choice Means Segregation. *Kappan (101)*5, 40–43. https://doi.org/10.1177/0031721720903827.

Shields, L., Newman, A., and Satz, D. (2017, Summer). Equality of Educational Opportunity. In: E. N. Zalta, ed., *The Stanford Encyclopedia of Philosophy.* Retrieved from https://plato.stanford.edu/archives/sum2017/entries/equal-ed-opportunity.

Skinner, R. R. (2019, July 23). *State and Local Financing of Public Schools.* Washington, DC: Congressional Research Service.

Snow, D., and Burke, B. (2019, Spring/Summer). The Practice of State Budgeting in Massachusetts: The Long-Term Effects of Structural Imbalance. *Municipal Finance Journal (40)*1–2, 77–100.

Spady, W. G. (1994). *Outcome Based Education: Critical Issues and Answers.* Arlington, VA: American Association of School Administrators.

States News Service. (2019, May 20). Charter School Founder and CEO Sentences to 2'[*sic*] Years in Federal Prison for Misappropriating $3.2 Million in Public Education Funds. *States News Service.*

Sternberg, R. J. (2017, Sep 11). Testing: For Better and Worse. *Phi Delta Kappan.* Retrieved from https://doi.org/10.1177/0031721716681780.

Stewart, M. S., and Moon, J. S. (2016a, October). Follow the Money: A Comprehensive Review of the Funding Mechanisms of Voucher Programs in Six Cases. CEEP Research Brief. Bloomington, IN: Indiana University School of Education.

———. (2016b, October). Understanding How School Vouchers Are Funded: Summary of Funding for Ohio's Cleveland Scholarship and EdChoice Programs. CEEP Research Brief. Bloomington, IN: Indiana University School of Education.

Stillings-Candal, C., and Ardon, K. (2019, February). Charter Public School Funding in Massachusetts: A Primer. (Policy Brief). Boston, MA: Pioneer Institute Public Policy Research.

Stratford, M. (2020, January 22). Montana School Choice Case before the Supreme Court today. *POLITICO Morning Education.* Retrieved from www.politico.com/morning-education/2020/01/22

Sugimoto, T. J. (2016). *Analysis of the 2015–2017 Indiana School Funding Formula.* Bloomington, IN: Center for Evaluation & Education Policy.

Suitts, S. (2016, November). Students Facing Poverty: The New Majority. *Educational Leadership (74)*3, 36–40.

———. (2019, June 4). Segregationists, Libertarians, and the Modern "School Choice" Movement. Monograph. *Southern Spaces.* Retrieved from www.southern spaces.org.

Swensson, J., and Shaffer, M. (2020). *Defining the Good School: Educational Adequacy Is More Than Minimums.* London: Rowman & Littlefield.

Swensson, J., Ellis, J., and Shaffer, M. (2019a). *Unraveling Reform Rhetoric: What Educators Need to Know and Understand.* London: Rowman & Littlefield.

———. (2019b). *An Educator's GPS: Fending off the Free Market of Schooling for America's Students.* London: Rowman & Littlefield.

Toland, J. C. (2016). *Public School Finance Decoded: A Straightforward Approach to Linking the Budget to Student Achievement.* London: Rowman & Littlefield.

Totenberg, N. (2020, January 23). Supreme Court Could Be Headed to a Major Unraveling of Public School Funding. *NPR.* Retrieved from https://www.npr.org /2020/01/23798668729/supreme-court-could-be-headed-to-a-major-unraveling-of -public-school-funding.

Ujifusa, A. (2019, June 29). Koch Network Announces New Education Lobbying Group, Walton Funding Pact. *(BLOG). Education Week.* Retrieved from www .edweek.org/Ujifusa.2019/06

US Government Accountability Office (GAO). (2016, August). Private School Choice Programs Are Growing and Can Complicate Providing Certain Federally Funded Services to Eligible Students. *GAO Highlights.* Retrieved from GAO-16-712.

———. (2018, February). Department of Education: Resource and Achievement Trends. *Report to the Committee on Homeland Security and Governmental Affairs, U.S. Senate.* Retrieved from GAO-18-154.

Villanueva, C. (2018a, March). Investing in Our Future: What You Need to Know as Texas Re-Examines the School Finance System. *Center for Public Policy Priorities.*

———. (2018b, August). Investing in Our Future: What You Need to Know as Texas Re-examines the School Finance System. *Center for Public Policy Priorities.*

———. (2019, January). Charter School Funding: A Misguided Growing State Responsibility. *Center for Public Policy Priorities.* Retrieved from https://every texan.org/images/EO_2019_CharterSchoolFunding.pdf.

Vincent, W. S. (1945). *Emerging Patterns of Public School Practice.* New York: Bureau of Publications, Teachers College, Columbia University.

Vowell, S. (2020, Feb 18). School Choice Logic Doesn't Apply Here. Does the Supreme Court Get That? *The New York Times.* Retrieved from https://www.nytimes .com/2020/02/18/opinion/supreme-court.

Waddington, R. J., and Berends, M. (2018). Impact of the Indiana Choice Scholarship Program: Achievement Effects for Students in Upper Elementary and Middle School. *Journal of Policy Analysis and Management (37)*4, 783–808. doi:10.1002 /pam.22086.

Weathers, E. S., and Sosina, V. E. (2019). Separate Remains Unequal: Contemporary Segregation and Racial Disparities in School District Revenue. (CEPA Working

Paper No. 19-02). Stanford, CA: Center for Education Policy Analysis. Retrieved from http://cepa.stanford.edu/wp19-02.

Weaver, H. L. (2018, January 30). What Donald Trump, Mike Pence, and Betsy DeVos Won't Tell You about "School Choice." *Speak Freely.* Washington, DC: ACLU. Retrieved from https://www.aclu.org/blog/religious-liberty/religion-and -public-schools/what-donald-trump-mike-pence-and-betsy-devos-wont

Wolf, P. J., Cheng, A., Batdorff, M., Maloney, L., May, J. F., and Speakman, S. T. (2014). The Productivity of Public Charter Schools. (School Choice Demonstration Project). Fayetteville: University of Arkansas. Retrieved from www.uaedreform .org/the-productivity-of-charter-schools.

Wood, R. C. (2019, Spring). Charter School Constitutional Funding Challenges: North Carolina and Texas May Serve as Harbingers for the Future. *Journal of Education Finance (44)*4, 341–60.

Wright, C. (2017, June 20). Charter School Exec Is Charged; He Is Accused of Using More than $1 Million in Public Funds for Personal Expenses. *Tampa Bay Times.* GALEIA495963636

Index

ALEC. *See* American Legislative
    Exchange Council
CCSS. *See* Common Core State
    Standards
EMO. *See* Educational Management
    Organization
ESEA. *See* Elementary and Secondary
    Education Act
NAEP. *See* National Assessment of
    Educational Progress
NCLB. *See* No Child Left Behind Act
ROI. *See* Return On Investment
SFR. *See* School Finance Reform

65% Solution, 38–39

accountability, 21, 55, 72, 89, 104
    Accountable-For, 55–56, 140
    Accountable-To, 55–56, 64, 86, 140,
    142, 153
    operational, 21
    outcome, 21, 147
achievement, 19, 59, 72, 85–86, 98,
    127, 129, 152
    funding for, 70, 72, 116
    gap, 82, 90–91
adequacy, 9, 13, 25, 49, 115–116, 134,
    146

American Legislative Exchange Council
    (ALEC), 37, 47
Articles of Confederation, 79–81,
    97

"better," 17, 26, 64, 78–79, 81, 85–86,
    92, 101, 133–135, 139
bifurcation, 49, 69, 78, 81, 89, 111, 118,
    126, 137–138, 140
Brown v. Board, 80

charter schools (*see* privatization
    education)
choice education (*see* privatization
    education)
Common Core State Standards (CCSS),
    98
common good, 18, 27, 96, 105, 136,
    142, 147–148, 151
    non-excludable, 18, 144
    non-rival, 18, 144
competition, 60–61, 130–131, 134
cost, 11, 22, 27, 53, 64, 123, 125
    effectiveness, 66
    reduction, 54, 65, 98, 117, 147
court
    cases, 25–26, 95
    decisions, 26, 73, 103, 148

state, 25, 68, 70, 73
US Supreme, 27, 105, 119
Covid-19, 43, 69

democracy, 18, 28, 84, 127, 135
discrimination, 52, 61, 83, 114, 128
disparities, 65, 72, 92, 115, 122, 125, 137, 143, 151
dualities, 75, 80, 143, 150
dynamic instruction. *See* instruction

education, 78
 as a commodity, 97–98, 100–101, 121
 major perspectives of, 90, 125, 129
 original power of, 116
 purpose for, 145
educational gerrymandering, 46, 94, 117, 131
Educational Management Organization (EMO), 23, 54, 65, 99
efficiency, 13, 61, 65, 113, 144
Elementary and Secondary Education Act (ESEA), 7, 58
equity, 9, 12, 22–24, 107, 123, 125–126, 140
evolving hybrid, 133–134

foundation formula (*see* funding formula)
free market theory, 14, 22, 28, 32–33, 52, 66, 84–85, 96, 130, 144
 mechanisms, 22, 52, 90
 perspective, 16, 54, 85, 102
funding
 as input, 12, 107
 as output, 12, 107
 chaos, 69–70, 75
 degradation zone, 117, 119–121, 149
 disconnection, 72
 distribution, 5, 12, 19, 71, 109–110, 141
 effort, 5, 15
 flat, 11

level, 5, 12, 19, 23
 oversight, 73–74, 132, 141
 per-pupil, 127, 148
 progressive, 11
 regressive, 11, 110
 sectarian purposes for, 120
 source, 5, 24
 sufficiency, 12–13, 75, 153
funding formula, 6–8, 28, 45, 49, 121, 139
 impact on instruction, 19–20, 71, 132
 intentions of, 56–57
 manipulation of, 71, 117, 119, 122
 problems with, 17

Great Recession, 40, 69, 103

ideology, 77, 90, 102, 131, 142, 145
 essentialism, 83
 individualism, 83
impermanence, 96–97, 114, 144
inequity, 8–9, 72, 109, 121, 127, 152
instruction, 16, 19, 50–51, 71, 145
 dynamic, 70, 107, 114–115, 133–134, 141, 149
 payment for, 57
 test prep, 55, 88
instructional program (*see* instruction)
intentional impermanence, 93
interdependence, 151–153
investment, 11, 51, 59, 64

Lancasterian Method, 120
laws (*see* state statutes)
legislators (*see* state legislatures)

management, 66, 133
 new public, 96, 114, 150

National Assessment of Educational Progress (NAEP), 26, 51, 54, 66, 92, 129, 149
No Child Left Behind Act (NCLB), 33, 88

path dependence, 109, 114, 117, 132–133, 141
Potemkin Village, 67, 75
poverty, 81–82, 89, 115, 149
preference substitution, 19, 47, 140
privatization education, 13, 16, 34, 45, 70, 73, 87, 101–102, 104, 114, 130, 136
  for-profit, 52–53, 65, 84, 99, 128, 142, 144
  funding for, 20, 42, 57–58, 118
  intentions of, 79, 120, 128
  mechanisms of, 52–53, 90, 144
productivity, 63, 65–67, 96
public good (*see* common good)
public sector, 79, 64, 81, 96, 111, 120, 124, 143–144

racism, 81–83, 89, 114, 119
referendum, 41
reform, 68, 73, 116, 135
  resource–free, 47
Return On Investment (ROI), 59, 66–67, 113, 148
revenue, 60, 65, 69–70, 88, 140, 148

school districts, 59
  high-minority enrollment, 41
  high-poverty (*see* low-wealth)
  high-wealth, 24, 110, 140
  low-minority enrollment, 41
  low-poverty (*see* high-wealth)
  low-wealth, 22, 24, 51, 110–111, 140
School Finance Reform (SFR), 51, 64, 148–149
segregation academies, 80
spending, 22, 91, 106
  on instruction, 91

standards, 33, 36
standardized testing, 85–88, 112, 132, 146–147
  cost of, 89
state
  constitution, 6, 10, 25–26, 48, 90, 134, 140, 150
  legislatures, 10, 13, 22–23, 26, 32, 46, 68, 94, 113, 128, 151
students, 9–10, 18, 49, 55, 72, 82, 97, 107, 128–129, 138, 142–143

tax
  base, 4
  cuts, 70
  elasticity, 4, 12, 140
  federal, 7
  local, 5, 23
  property, 6, 14, 20, 71, 103, 137
  rate, 4, 23, 118
  sales, 6–7
  state, 6, 24
  yield, 4
taxpayers, 9, 27, 58, 70, 125, 133
third-party entity, 23, 73
traditional public education, 6, 15–16, 18, 23, 45, 50–51, 79, 104

underfunding, 11, 14, 41, 52, 59–60, 94, 106, 111, 113, 117–118, 125, 150–151

virtual education (*see* privatization education)
virtual school (*see* privatization education)

About the Authors

John Ellis, PhD, served public education across Indiana as an educator in K–16 public education. His extensive experience in diverse school communities as a teacher, school leader, district leader, and assistant professor gives him a perspective enriched by innumerable opportunities for learningful conversations. His scholar and practitioner interests include school leadership, quality school practices, and traditional public education.

Lynn Lehman, EdD, currently serves as the representative from Ball State University on the University Superintendent Search Team. He recently transitioned from a full-time appointment as an Assistant Professor in the Department of Educational Leadership. His career reflects dedication to diverse students and communities while serving as a teacher, assistant principal, principal, deputy superintendent, and superintendent.

Jeff Swensson, PhD, served for forty-five years as an educator in K–16 public education. Throughout a career as a teacher, building leader, and district leader in urban and suburban school districts, he learned from dedicated and talented colleagues about the value of positive liberty and principled reasoning.

Made in the USA
Monee, IL
07 August 2024

63345050R10111